PÁDRAIG McCARTHY

How to
STOP
GAMBLING
in 30+1 days.

A 30+ 1 day gambling recovery guide for use by gamblers, addiction counsellors and partners of problem gamblers.

All rights reserved. No part of this publication may be reproduced or transmitted in any form or by any means, electronic or mechanical, including photocopy, recording, or any information storage or retrieval system, without prior permission in writing from the publisher.

No responsibility or liability is assumed by the publisher or author for any injury, damage, or financial loss sustained to persons or property from the use of this information, personal or otherwise, either directly or indirectly. While every effort has been made to ensure reliability and accuracy of the information, external websites, e-mail addresses, research findings, and phone numbers within, all liability, negligence, or otherwise, from any use, misuse, or abuse of the operation of any methods, strategies, techniques, instructions, or ideas contained in the material herein, is the sole responsibility of the reader.

Important Disclaimer

All information is generalised, presented for informational purposes only, not medical advice, and presented "as is" without warranty or guarantee of any kind. Readers are cautioned not to rely on this information as medical advice and to consult a qualified medical, psychiatric, dietary, fitness, or other appropriate professional for their specific needs.

Copyright © 2016 **Pádraig McCarthy**
All rights reserved.
Revised edition.

ISBN: **1491004134**
ISBN 13: **9781491004135**

If you gamble

You may be in the mire of a gambling addiction, you may be gambling and wondering if you have a problem or you may have stopped gambling and would like help. If any of these is the case, this book will aim to help you. If you have picked up this book and believe you are fully in control of your gambling, then please put it back on the shelf and continue spending your time unproductively gambling. If you are in any way coerced into buying this book or have no real intention to stop gambling, then please put the book back on the shelf and continue your life of destructive gambling. However, if you do want to stop gambling, I will share with you a revolutionary approach that will help quell the urge to gamble within thirty days.

If you are a spouse, partner, friend, or family member of a gambler

You may have a partner or friend who you deem may have a gambling problem. If you are not sure how to broach the subject, you want to help but do not know how, or you do not understand what the world of a gambler is like, then this book will help you identify behaviours and attitudes of problem gamblers and ways you can help steer the gambler towards the path of recovery. There is a whole chapter dedicated to people like you who want to help problem gamblers, and the rest of the book will help you understand the dynamics, consequences, and causes of gambling addiction, as well as the detailed recovery programme that you can work through with the problem gambler.

If you are a gambling therapist

While you may have developed your own strategy and therapeutic approach for problem and pathological gamblers, there may be other insights and approaches in this recovery programme that you can use in your day-to-day dealings with problem gamblers.

PREFACE

My name is Pádraig McCarthy. I was a problem gambler; today I am free from the gambling addiction. Gambling addiction brought me to my knees, brought intense emotional strain into my life, and brought poverty to my door. However, I fought back; I used various techniques, tools, and strategies to quell the urges, and to deal competently and effectively with the emotional, relationship, and financial obstacles that I encountered. I am going to share these techniques with you in this book.

In spite of my gambling addiction, I had a relatively successful academic and work career. This may sound anomalous and contradictory, but the picture presented does not reflect the whole story. While I was relatively successful in academia and employment, I was simultaneously sliding down a spiral of destruction to a dark abyss, where only pain, hopelessness, depression, anxiety, desperation, and financial pain existed.

I managed to hide my addiction from those closest to me. There was no reason to expect anything. I was a college graduate, in a good job, and doing well. To all and sundry, I seemed like a level-headed, confident, and career-minded guy with everything going for him. However, reality was different. I had accumulated large debts, left a trail of broken relationships, encountered physical ill-health, put myself under intense emotional and financial stress, and prevented myself from achieving my full potential in life and work due to the grasp of a gambling addiction.

I stopped gambling on April 3, 2008. I have not gambled since; I have no desire to gamble today and plan never to gamble again. The journey through recovery is not easy, but it is so rewarding, enjoyable, and utterly liberating. Gambling took not only my money from me but also my time, time that could have been spent doing productive, happy, and rewarding things.

My life is good today. I am happy, I have a rewarding and challenging job, I have worked hard to reduce my debt, and I appreciate fully all that life has to offer. I have taken up new sports, new hobbies, new studies, and I surround myself with people who bring me great joy and inspiration.

I want to give back what I have learned on my road to recovery to all gamblers who really want to stop gambling. Gamblers who are sick of losing money and tired of running and hiding from creditors, gamblers who can no longer take the pain of deceiving and hurting those closest to them, gamblers who are tired of feeling depressed and anxious due to time and money lost to gambling, and want to be liberated from the prison without walls that is a gambling addiction.

I hope this book will be the key to your freedom. I want you to regain that person you left behind when you started on your gambling journey. I believe if you give this recovery programme everything you've got, you will regain the confidence, positivity, financial stability, and happiness that you so richly deserve. Go for it, and do not wait any longer; a far happier, more rewarding, and more enriching life awaits.

CONTENTS

Preface v

PART I

Chapter 1 Overview of Gambling 3
    1.1   Introduction 3
    1.2   What is gambling? 9
    1.3   Why do we gamble? 10
    1.4   Effects of gambling addiction 15
    1.5   Treatment available for gamblers 18
    1.6   Home truths about gambling 20
    1.7   Gambling myths 25
    1.8   Am I a pathological or problem gambler? 29
    1.9   Types of gamblers 32
        1.9.1   Tom's story: online gambler 33
        1.9.2   Peter's story: scratch card and lotto addict 34
        1.9.3   Jim's story: casino addict 35
        1.9.4   Ann's story: bingo addict 37

Chapter 2 Programme Introduction 39
    2.1   Introduction 39

Chapter 3 Phase One: STABILITY 43
    3.1   Introduction 43
    3.2   Phase one goals and objectives 43
    3.3   Phase one overview 44
    3.4   Coping techniques for phase one "Stability" 45
        3.4.1   Recommended coping techniques 46
        3.4.2   Suggested coping techniques 50
    3.5   Urge Suppression Techniques 53
        3.5.1   Gambling process 54

3.5.2 Dealing with the urge to place a bet · · · · · · · · · · · · · · · 55
3.5.3 What are these techniques? · 56
   Technique one · 57
   Technique two · 58
3.5.4 Dealing with general gambling urges · · · · · · · · · · · · · · 59
3.6 Summary of phase one · 61

Chapter 4 Phase Two: ACCEPTANCE 65
4.1 Introduction · 65
4.2 Objectives of phase two · 66
4.3 Recommended coping techniques for phase two · · · · · · 69

Chapter 5 Phase Three: FUNCTIONING and ECONOMY 75
5.1 Introduction · 75
5.2 Goals of phase three · 78
5.3 Coping with moods and negative emotions · · · · · · · · · · 79
   5.3.1 Coping techniques for moods and negative emotions · · 80
5.4 Coping with financial pressures · 89
   5.4.1 Coping techniques for managing debt · · · · · · · · · · · · · · 90
5.5 Coping with legal issues · 95
   5.5.1 Coping strategies in dealing with legal issues · · · · · · · · 96
5.6 Dealing with problems · 97
   5.6.1 Coping techniques in dealing with problems · · · · · · · · · 98
5.7 Dealing with irrational thinking · · · · · · · · · · · · · · · · · · · 102
   5.7.1 Coping strategies in dealing with irrational thinking · · · 103

PART II

Chapter 6 Pillars 107
6.1 Introduction · 107
   6.1.1 Scenario one · 109
   6.1.2 Scenario two · 110
6.2 Pillar development · 111
   6.2.1 Emotional pillar · 111
   6.2.2 Physical pillar · 113

6.2.3	Spiritual pillar	115
6.2.4	Financial pillar	116
6.2.5	Personal development pillar	117
6.2.6	Social network pillar	118
6.2.7	Relationship pillar	119

Chapter 7 Help for Partners, Friends, or Family of a Gambling Addict 123

7.1	Introduction	123
7.2	Stages of stopping	124
7.3	Gambling behaviours	126
7.4	Dealing with problem gamblers	128
7.5	Coping techniques in dealing with problem gamblers	129

Chapter 8 The Future 133

Appendix 1	Daily Diary Template	139
Appendix 2	Financial Summary Template	141
Appendix 3	Managing Urges Template	143
Appendix 4	Problem-Solving Worksheet	146
Appendix 5	Benefit Analysis Sheet	148
Appendix 6	Emotional Analysis Worksheet	149
Appendix 7	List of Organisations in Ireland, UK, United States and Australia	151

This book is dedicated to all those who have been with me through my journey of recovery. Special thanks to Tom F, Johnny G and Nuala K for their unstinting and unconditional support. To my Mam, Nan, family, Aggie and my good friends, special thanks to Catherine B, Brian G, Dave M, Loretto and Nigel, who were there for me when I needed their support most. A big thank you too to Barry McD for his inspiration and guidance in helping me get this project off the ground, to all those who have lent their encouragement and expertise in the writing of this book, and to recovering gambling addicts everywhere.

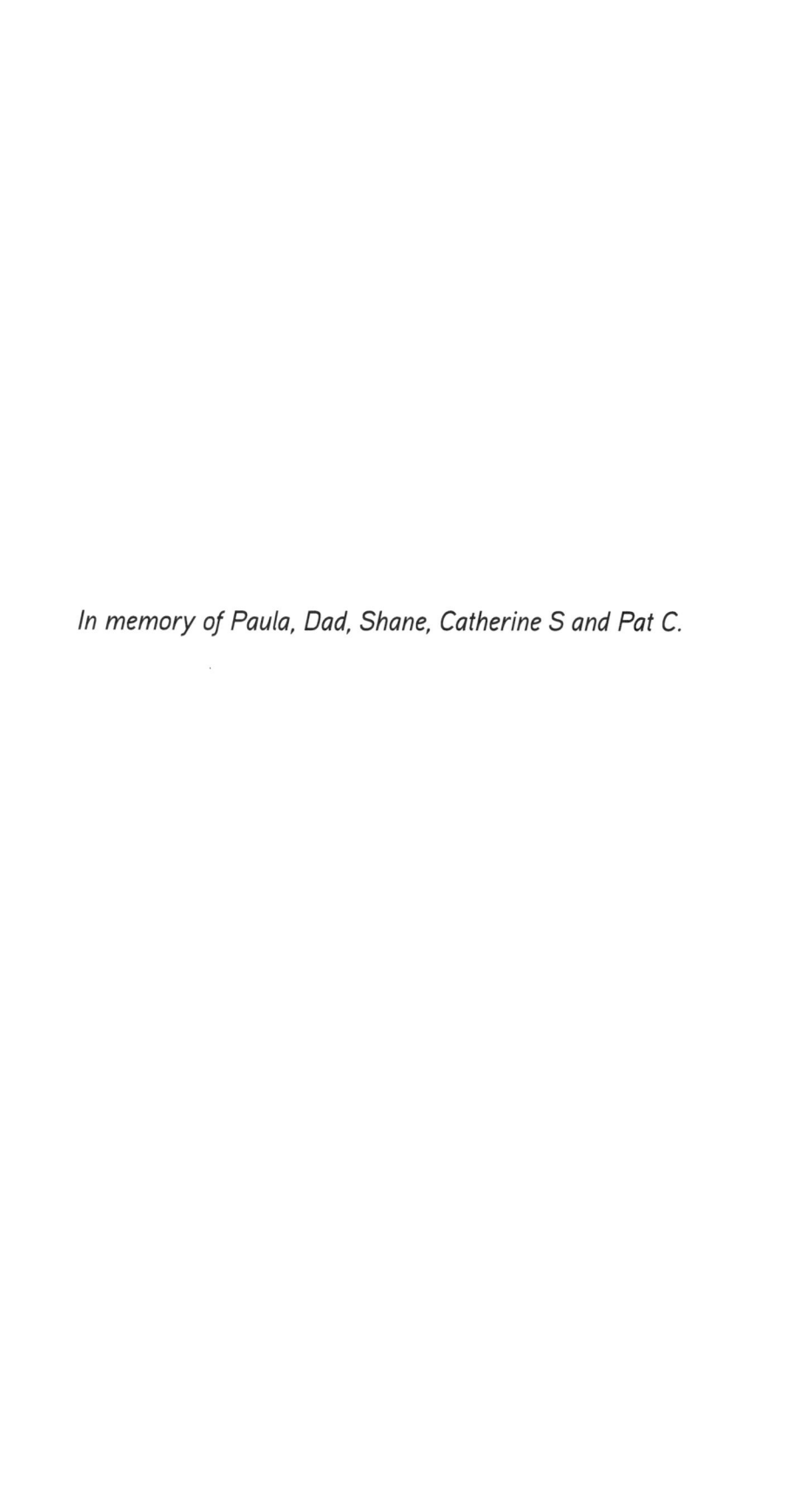

In memory of Paula, Dad, Shane, Catherine S and Pat C.

'No longer yourself,
your mind will be owned and steered
from elsewhere now.
You will sacrifice anything
to dance once more
to the haunted music with your fatal beloved
who owns the eyes to your heart'

  Verse from the poem *For an Addict* by John O'Donohue

PART I

CHAPTER 1
Overview of Gambling

1.1 Introduction

Heart palpitating, clenching my betting slip in a vice-like grip, I will my horse home with all my being. The winning line draws closer, a head-bopping finish, adrenaline courses through my veins, just pipped on the line—again. I look around in disbelief at the indifferent punters. I pointlessly shout expletives at the jockey for his ineptitude, but he does not hear. My legs wobble at thought of losing all my money. I feel as if I am detached from reality. Why am I here in this den of iniquity?

I barge out of the bookmaker's, grasping my set of keys, and slowly embed the car key into the palm of my hand; the physical pain is a temporary relief from the mental pain, the utter dismay and anger at myself for draining my wallet, once again, of the bundle of one hundred, fifty, and twenty euro notes that it contained that morning. A tornado of thoughts swirl around in my head, every sinew of my body twitching and convulsing in unison with each thought of how I relentlessly gambled every euro I had earlier by betting on every greyhound and horse race, not to mention the virtual racing that is churned up to fill the gaps between live racing. Why? Oh why? Oh why did I go to the bookies this morning? The frenetic rush earlier to withdraw the maximum amount I could from the ATM, before the direct debit for the car repayment came out of my bank account that evening, another direct debit to be returned. Why did I not leave when I was winning? The jockey was at fault; why did he not go wide and avoid his run being blocked? Beaten a short head for all my money back; this is surreal. Will the car have enough petrol to get me home? Rent money spent, barely enough to buy something to eat this evening.

More lies to those closest to me, the incessant questions that will ensue, the aloofness I will adopt to hide my pain, more mood swings, my irritability as a result of people asking me where I was all day. Scrambling to get a loan, I will concoct more lies, a phone call to a mate to see if he can transfer one hundred euros to my account. I just want to curl up in bed and let the pain subside, let the chaos reign in the chaotic world that I have created. Wave upon wave of emotion pulsates through my body—anger, despondency, fear mixed with a feeling of impending doom—and my mind races uncontrollably with irrational and dark thoughts.

Then serenity overcomes me, my mind calms, and a false composure pervades. "This is a temporary setback; tomorrow is a new day. I can borrow a couple hundred and will win back today's losses—easy." And so the cycle of madness continues, a self-perpetuating spiral of destruction that contaminates every part of my life: my work, my relationships, my social life, and my health, both physical and mental. It is a prison without walls where you feel like a spectator to the world whirring past you; the grasp of the compulsion to gamble is overwhelming. I say each day that "it is my last day of gambling," yet the gravitational pull of the bookie shop is too great; it seduces me with its false sense of comfort and security where I can while away a few hours and leave my troubles behind.

The rush to get the first of many bets on, the veneer of happiness that covers my deep-seated anguish and pain. Today feels good; I fancy a few good things later on the card. Today is going to be my day. But it never is my day. I may win money some days, but I lose time. I lose time that could be spent on productive activities like exercising, reading, walking with loved ones, going to college, hiking, writing, learning a musical instrument—the list is endless. The monetary loss compounds my temporal loss; it takes a huge toll on my mental and emotional well-being. I can no longer take this, but I cannot stop. The madness keeps me sane.

The above anecdote was a typical heavy betting day for me in my twenty years of gambling—the gradual decline to a hellish, dark abyss from where I thought no escape was possible. I could spend twenty chapters detailing similar and yet more chaotic stories filled with deception, the destruction of relationships, dereliction of my personal development, mental anguish, spiralling debt, sleeplessness, depression, despair, and the utter loss of control. It was like, as Bruce Springsteen wrote, "a freight train running through the middle of my head," yet I was maintaining the facade of "all is well" to those closest to me.

I recall my first bet being in my early teens. I used to place my cross doubles and cross treble bets with the local bookmaker, under the pretence that they were for my father. I was only the messenger, well so the local bookie thought. I used to rush home and wait with abated breath and eager anticipation to watch the races being broadcast on the TV. In those days, racing on TV was confined mainly to Saturdays and the big race meetings such as Aintree, Cheltenham, Ascot, and Goodwood. The excitement of watching your horse finish first passed the post was something I never experienced before, I wanted more. The seeds were sown. As I progressed through my teens and twenties, the frequency and amount I bet increased steadily. Horse racing, dog racing, slot machines, scratch cards, lotto and poker machines were, primarily, the betting mediums I gambled on. Any extra money I earned was used to fund my gambling. The emergence of racing channels and the daily coverage of every horse and dog race in the UK and Ireland, and eventually European and US races, was music to my ears. I could not get enough of it. I was sure I had the skill, expertise, and know-how to make a lot of money by gambling. An illusion that accompanied me during all of my years of gambling.

I would structure my days around gambling. Family, college, work, social life, sports, and relationships, while very important to me, took second place, an inconvenience and distraction in my pursuit of my dream to make millions from gambling. I would concoct stories and lies to cover and hide the financial losses incurred from the time spent wantonly gambling. Gambling, especially in college, was a social thing where I would go to the bookmakers with college friends. It seemed like a rite of passage, and for most of my friends gambling never became a problem, but it caught a hold of me and did eventually become a big problem.

Gambling served as a distraction, an escape from the trials and tribulations of life, an escape from me. I would become totally immersed in the activity of gambling, the dissection of the form guides, the detailed discussions with friends on who would be sure to win the big race that day, the banter and fun, that slowly turned to pain and loss, the adrenaline rush in the excitement of winning or near wins, regaling people with the anecdotes of the wins, near wins and losses of that day's racing, it defined who I was, it became a way of life.

As I progressed in my career, the more money I earned, the greater the size and frequency of my bets. I would have no problem putting a large bet, the equivalent of a months' salary, on a horse if I was sure of his credentials and chances. The opportunities to bet increased significantly, there was the opportunity to gamble almost every minute of the day, from dog racing, horse racing, lotto draws, virtual horse and dog racing, evening racing, all forms of sport betting, scratch cards, casino, poker tournaments, it was a never ending carousel of gambling options.

I cannot think of a day in my twenty plus years of gambling that I would not at least think about putting a bet on. My moods oscillated in line with whether I won or lost. I recall the days of heavy losses and putting on a veneer of being cool, calm and collected to my family, friends, girlfriends, and work colleagues, while simultaneously being totally distraught, demoralised, deflated, remorseful, guilty, angry, ashamed and disbelieving at what I had done. However, I would quickly forget about any heavy losses, put it down to being unlucky, and that my luck would turn.

I had big wins, but I would invariably gamble the winnings and a lot more besides within a short period of time. This would only add to my despair. I borrowed heavily to support my gambling; this was in spite of earning very good salaries; working for different companies within the Information Technology industry. I estimate that I lost in excess of €350,000 in my twenty plus years of gambling. This figure would include income earned, and subsequently lost, and loans (personal and institutional) received.

Any personal relationships I had were severely impacted by my gambling. I was never able to commit wholeheartedly to any relationship, the problems compounded by my long absences away gambling in bookie shops, the lies concocted to hide any traces of my gambling, the financial strain, the low moods, and depression that would accompany bouts of heavy losses. I managed to keep my career on track, but just about. I knew I needed to fund my gambling and a good salary facilitated that. I really enjoyed my work, and like my personal relationships, never gave it my full attention and would have foregone many career opportunities as a result.

In spite of heavy losses, lost relationships, depression, financial devastation, and the detrimental impact gambling had on every facet of my life, I continued to gamble. In the end, I am not even sure if I liked gambling, it was soul destroying. In fact, I lost interest in almost everything; I got little enjoyment from anything other than gambling, the one thing that took everything from me, that was the craziness of it. I so badly wanted to stop but the draw of the bookmakers or casino was too great, I had to satisfy the urge, I had to give in to the lure of gambling, the seductive promises of big wins that never came, the pipe dream, the illusion of clearing all my debts and worries with one big win, the one big win that never had, would or will come.

The financial pressure became so intense, I could not sleep, I could not concentrate on my work, and my credit rating took a hammering, to such an extent that recourse to bank loans was and is no longer an option for me. I borrowed from friends and family under false pretences. The downward spiral to complete desperation, desolation and destruction came to a shuddering thump on April 3rd 2008, when I walked into a Gamblers Anonymous meeting in Dublin. That day I started a new chapter of my life. I reached out for help because I had my fill of losing money and deceiving those closest to me. I had my fill of dealing with creditors. I had my fill of constant anxiety, depression and sleeplessness. I yearned for normality. I was afraid of what was happening to me and how little control I had over my gambling behaviour and the looming problems that were getting worse by the week. I wanted to be in the company of people that understood the pain I was enduring and could help me on my journey to recovery. I had a lot to offer the world and I was determined to fulfil my potential, and that can only be done free from the shackles of a gambling addiction. Many former gambling addicts I know are highly intelligent, witty, charismatic people with great entrepreneurial spirit and who, once they overcame their addiction, used their abilities and skills to build very successful businesses and careers. Since I stopped gambling I have not looked back and while the road is not smooth, I am going in the right direction, and the views on the way are spectacular. Come and join me on the journey.

If you are gambling heavily today, then most things I have mentioned will resonate with you. It feels as if your mind is clogged up with the tar of ill thoughts, the whirlwind of emotions, and the despondency and chaos that defines and invades your life. Yes, life is horrible right now, I will not try to insist otherwise but there is hope, there is a solution, and there is a way out of your hell. I have come through and you will too, if you really want to. I will state honestly that the journey will be a challenge, but it will be enjoyable; yes, you read that correctly—enjoyable. Right now, this may seem crazy, but bear with me and all will be revealed. So let's begin the journey.

1.2 What is gambling?

Gambling is an old age activity that is a form of entertainment where there is voluntary participation by two or more parties; where a wager of money or item of material value on an event, of unknown certainty, is made; the outcome of which determines the redistribution of money or valuable items wagered, or in some cases, the outcome of event could result in a promise to do something by the losing participant. Gambling can be traced back as far as Egyptian times 4000BC. Many historical texts refer to various forms of wagering that existed in Europe during the Dark Ages. More recently, advances in technology such as online betting, the ever increasing number of events and games to gamble on, and the sprawl of gambling outlets such as bookmakers, casino's, bingo halls, poker tournaments, lotteries, and so on makes gambling readily accessible and available to everyone. Gambling can be found in almost every race and culture in the world today.

With the bewildering array of gambling mediums to wager on today, it is almost impossible to categorise them accurately. However, four main categories of legal gambling can be identified, namely:

- Gaming: the exchange of money on the outcome of a game e.g., poker, roulette, slots, blackjack, and so on.
- Betting: wagering on the outcome of a future event such as horse racing, football, other sporting events, elections etc.
- Lotteries: bingo, scratch cards, lotto and so on.
- Speculation: gambling on share prices, business investments, property etc.

Gambling can take primarily two forms. First form is continuous in nature i.e. there is a very short delay between the placing of the bet and knowing the outcome; this could be seconds, minutes or hours. Examples of continuous forms of gambling are horse racing, roulette, slots, fruit machines, poker, blackjack, and so on. The other form of gambling is discontinuous in nature, where there is a delay between the placing of the bet and outcome, and the event is held infrequently. Examples of discontinuous forms of gambling are lottery draws, raffles, etc. There are far more levels of risk associated with continuous forms of gambling and more chance of impaired control.

1.3 Why do we gamble?

Why do we gamble and how does it take hold of our lives?

This is a question I have posed to myself throughout my gambling years. It still baffles me to this day how gambling took a hold of me and that I persisted to gamble in spite of mounting losses, intense stress, negative impacts on my work and working relationships, corrosive damage to personal relationships, and the toll on my physical, emotional, and mental well-being.

In his book *The Power of Now*, Eckhart Tolle states that "Every addiction is caused by the refusal to accept your pain," indeed, it may be suggested here that the pain of losing hides a deeper pain. Is addiction the symptom, and not the cause, of the deeper pain? I have heard people say that "gamblers like losing," and as irrational and perverse as that sounds, it may well hold some truth. Indeed, when gambling, the "near misses," in many cases, cause more of a thrill than the actual winning itself. This may be the reason problem gamblers gamble even more after losing on previous bets. Some gamblers are egotistical, domineering, controlling, and manipulative (many with low self-esteem), and feel they can "beat the system," which drives them on to gamble. Some gamblers feel others will deem them to have failed at gambling and therefore failed at life, this is irrational and erroneous thinking, so they continue to gamble to try and get that "big win" that never comes. Some gamblers feel that gambling gives them reprieve from interminable boredom and provides a social outlet to alleviate this boredom. Some gamblers gamble for the action and adrenaline rush it temporarily provides; some gamblers use gambling as a means of escape from reality, where reality is distorted, and stresses and negative emotions are repressed. Some gamblers gamble for the challenge and the sense of achievement they feel when they win. Some gamblers create an identity for themselves from gambling, such as "The Shrewd Gambler," which may be a reason for them to continue gambling. Some gamble for no other reason than to just gamble, plain and simple.

Gambling addiction does not discriminate on grounds of social class, ethnic background, economic status, demographics, geography, religion, age, or gender; it can afflict anyone. There is increasing recognition within gambling research that gambling problems lie on a continuum from pathological (disordered gambling) through compulsive, problem, at risk (moderate and low), and social (not a problem gambler). I refer in this guide primarily to pathological, now referred to as disordered gambling, and problem gamblers. But it is difficult to define or identify when a gambler's gambling is out of control and when he or she needs help. My answer here is simple: if time is wasted and gambling has negative effects, even at a low level, on his or her finances, relationships, work, career, or mental and emotional well-being, then he or she needs to stop gambling or seek help if unable to stop.

I am hesitant to apply the term "disease" to a gambling addiction for two reasons. First, a disease implies "no choice," that is, you do not choose to have a disease, and you are unable, in many cases, to alter its progression. Second, many gamblers use the excuse of "I am suffering from a disease and have no control over it," that gives them an excuse and reason to continue their gambling behaviour. They use the term "disease" to explain or justify, wrongly, their failure to control their addiction. I see gambling addiction as a dysfunctional behaviour that one chooses not to control or alter. My own view is that the real disease or pain is not the gambling addiction but the underlying condition such as depression, anxiety, personality or mood disorder, unresolved conflicts of the past, and so on. The gambling addiction medicates away, and helps in coping with, the underlying pain. I do think there are certain biochemical and neurochemical factors and the creation of brain reward circuits that play a part in gambling addiction. There may also be certain predisposing genetic factors that make some people more susceptible to pathological and problem gambling than others. But whether these factors cause gambling addiction or the gambling addiction was the cause of the biochemical changes or brain states is another issue entirely and a question for another day. Other studies have shown that gamblers have low levels of the hormone and neurotransmitter norepinephrine, which is secreted under stress, arousal, or thrill; these studies infer that pathological and problem gamblers gamble to make up for their under dosage. A research team from Caltech and University College London found that people with damaged amygdalae, an almond-shaped brain structure that plays a strong role in emotional regulation, showed a predilection to take risky behaviours that led to losing money.

I would like to add that from my own experiences, the anticipation of gambling and the near misses were as potent in compounding my gambling addiction as the winning itself. This may well be related to the brain circuitry and the chemical messaging mechanisms and dynamics of the brain; however, once I began the recovery process, the desire to gamble reduced over time. So were these desires conditioned because of gambling or genetically inherited? I cannot answer that, but if one can reduce or eliminate the desire to gamble by undertaking a recovery programme then it may not be that important ultimately.

The development of gambling addiction follows different trajectories, but there are some commonalities. According to the Illinois Institute for Addiction Recovery, there are four phases in gambling addiction:

- Winning phase: big wins and favourable view of gambling. Perceives himself or herself as almost professional. This phase typically lasts up to three to five years but could be longer.
- Losing phase: more preoccupation with gambling and impacts on finances, family, and work; there is "chasing" of losses where the gambler gambles more to win back losses. Accentuates and boasts about the wins but rarely, if ever, mentions the losses. Can last up to five years.
- Desperation phase: loses all control and cannot stop, accompanied by feelings of shame, guilt, self-hatred and fear. Spends every waking hour planning his or her gambling activities. Can last for months or years.
- Hopeless phase: loses all hope, does not care what happens, may commit crime to fund his or her gambling, becomes depressed, and may have suicidal tendencies.

In my research on the factors contributing to pathological and problem gambling, I have found a myriad of theories. In layman's terms the question is "Why do we continue to gamble in spite of our gambling behaviour causing us so many problems?" The theories encompass the following.

- Genetic factors: gambling or addiction genes passed on from parents or grandparents.
- Personality factors: impulsivity, sensation seeking, chasing adrenaline rushes, risk-taking, and so on.
- Emotional: gambling addicts may, in many cases, suffer from underlying emotional and mental health issues such as depression, anxiety, stress, anger, guilt, shame, and so on. Gambling medicates away the underlying pain which drives the gambler on to gamble in spite of gambling losses and the impact it has on family, partner, friends, work, relationships, mental, and emotional well-being.

- Erroneous beliefs and cognitions: perceived ability to predict outcome of events also known as the *"illusion of control,"* develops a *system* of betting or has lucky numbers that he or she plays on. Thinking becomes almost delusional; in some cases, the gambler can develop a personal relationship with a betting medium such as slot machine or poker machine, almost befriending the machine. Also includes irrational thinking e.g., series of losses means that a winning streak is near or that an object or lucky charm has power to help a gambler win on an event.
- Biological factors: chemical imbalances and dysfunctional operation of neurotransmitters (dopamine, serotonin, noradrenaline), depression, bipolar disorders, attention deficit disorder, personality and mood disorders, and so on. Gambling has been associated with the dopamine system in the brain, so gambling gives the gambler a euphoric feeling that can only be sustained by more gambling. Gambling behaviour changes the brain by making it hypersensitive to the deemed rewards of gambling; for a gambling addict, the brain considers gambling its only reward and only motivation, irrespective of the damaging and negative consequences.
- Sociological factors: exposure to gambling by other family members, friends, work colleagues, and so on may influence people to commence and maintain gambling. Gambling is seen as a social norm; you are assured your behaviour is normal by fellow gamblers, and this is further reinforced by the normalisation and detoxification, by the gaming industry, of gambling as a "harmless and fun activity." The almost ubiquitous presence of gambling venues and more recently the explosion of online gambling have made gambling readily accessible and available 24 x 7 that increases dramatically the incidence of problem gambling in society. Research has also indicated that the earlier people start and the greater the opportunity

to participate in gambling, they are more likely to develop a gambling addiction. Absence of education and life opportunities also make people more vulnerable to gambling addiction.
- Financial: As the gambling addict's financial situation deteriorates, he or she will assume, falsely, the only way to recover losses is to bet more and with larger amounts of money, known as *"chasing of losses."* This further compounds an already difficult situation and the gambler enters the desperate and hopelessness phase of gambling addiction.

It could well be one or a multitude of these factors that causes and maintains gambling addiction. We need to understand the reasons for pathological and problem gambling to ensure we provide appropriate treatment, and maybe one day can define behavioural markers in young people that indicate future gambling problems so we can put in place preventative measures to stop gambling addiction from developing. Maybe there is a force outside our consciousness that drives us to gamble uncontrollably. However, all I knew when I was gambling was that I could not stop, and theories on the causes of gambling addiction were far from my state of consciousness at that time. As a result, I have adopted the approach of dealing with the here and now, and I hope the coping techniques and tools that I provide will help problem and pathological gamblers stop gambling. This, it is hoped, will allow the gambler to address, in time, other issues in his or her life that may have contributed to or resulted from his or her gambling, such as depression, mood disorders, social interaction problems, bipolar disorder, personality disorder, and sociological issues.

1.4 Effects of gambling addiction

Gambling related problems span a wide area and can include relationship, financial, family, work, legal, physical, mental, and emotional. Some research points to the fact that gambling addiction has a much more serious downward spiral than other addictions, producing more severe, complex, and amount of negative problems and issues.

Some major effects of gambling addiction are outlined below:

- Depression: Clinical research has suggested that up to 75% of pathological gamblers suffer from symptoms of major depression such as low mood, low motivation, lack of concentration, sleep disturbance, irritability, loss of appetite, and feeling "blue". My own belief is that gambling is the symptom of an underlying psychological condition such as depression and this is exacerbated by the financial, work, relationship, and personal issues caused by the gambling addiction.
- Suicidal ideation: Gambling heavy and sustaining large losses will leave gamblers distressed, empty, remorseful, guilty, anxious, and fearful, especially if committed fraud to fuel his or her gambling. The depression, low mood, relationship problems, lack of clear thinking, and sense of hopelessness can result in problem gamblers having suicidal thoughts and ideas. In the United States, a report by the National Council on Problem Gambling showed approximately one in five pathological gamblers attempts suicide and anywhere up to 60% of pathological gamblers contemplate suicide. The Council also said that suicide rates amongst pathological gamblers are higher than for any other addictive disorder.
- Relationship breakdown: Time and money spent gambling can have very detrimental and damaging effects on the relationship(s) the gambler has with his or her spouse, partner, family, children, friends, work colleagues, manager and so on. As the gambler moves to the desperation phase of gambling addiction, lying and deceit becomes an automatic

part of everyday living. Deceit and lying are the hallmarks of many gambling addicts; this is necessary in order to hide the losses incurred or the fraud perpetuated to feed his or her gambling addiction.
- Financial ruin: Money is the raw material that fuels the gamblers addiction. It is inevitable that all avenues will be exhausted to ensure that the gambler gets access to funds to gamble. A gambler may recourse to illegal or fraudulent means to secure funds to gamble. The upshot is that gamblers may leave themselves bankrupt and in some cases open to criminal prosecution as a result of taking money fraudulently from a spouse, partner, friend or employer.
- Physical: The gambling addict's physical health may deteriorate rapidly as a consequence of the immense stress and anxiety of having to hide evidence of gambling losses, deal with relationship problems, cope with the stress of juggling work with the time needed to gamble, chasing losses, and trying to maintain normality in day-to-day living. Symptoms can include high blood pressure, exhaustion, gastro-intestinal problems, aches, pains, and headaches.
- Employment: Gambling addiction can have severe repercussions on the working life of the gambler. The effects can include absenteeism, reduced productivity, lack of concentration, and lacking motivation and initiative. The gambler may also be borrowing from colleagues and in some cases committing corporate fraud to feed his or her addiction.
- Criminality: Research has shown that 60% of pathological gamblers commit some criminal offence in order to support their gambling habits; about 22% are charged for offences. When all legal sources of funds have been exhausted, the only option is to commit a criminal offence to source the funds to feed his or her gambling addiction. The fraudulent behaviour can range from writing forged cheques, taking petty cash to

full scale embezzlement. The amount can vary from hundred to tens of thousands through to millions of euro.
- Social and economic costs: Excessive gambling in society produces social and economic costs such as criminality, poverty, family disintegration, reduced productivity, homelessness, and so on.

1.5 Treatment available for gamblers

While gambling, I believed the only recourse open to me was Gamblers Anonymous (GA) if I ever wanted to stop and get help for my gambling. GA is a twelve-step self-help support group for individuals experiencing gambling problems. I went to GA for the first year and a half of my recovery and have recommended GA in the thirty-day recovery programme. GA offers you a place where you can interact with fellow recovering problem gamblers, people who understand your pain and with whom you can talk openly. GA members are a great aid and support to each other. There is substantial clinical knowledge of the gambling addiction condition within GA and this is invaluable to those who have a true desire to stop gambling. Members offer solid advice and strategies for coping with immediate and pressing problems. On the flip side, the efficacy or success rate of GA—that is, members not gambling after one and two years—is rather low. Based on the low abstinence rate, it is evident that GA is not working for many people, and yet surprisingly it is still deemed, by many, to be the best way to recovery. I have my own views on why GA has a low success rate. One is that as a twelve-step programme that is very spiritually based, may be a step too far for many in the early stages of recovery. Another is that GA on its own may not address all the financial, social, personal, and psychological issues that recovering gambling addicts face. GA deems gambling addiction as a progressive illness and that the gambling addict is powerless over gambling. I tend to differ in opinion, in that I do not see gambling addiction as a progressive illness and the gambling addict still has the power to overcome his or her addiction, irrespective of what stage he or she is in. I would dearly like the GA fellowship to look at aspects of its approach and ideology, and how they can be improved or tweaked to address those areas that are not working, so that many more millions of people can benefit from the great work done by the Gamblers Anonymous fellowship throughout the world.

My approach is to offer a more holistic programme of recovery, one that includes attendance at GA meetings, but also uses aspects of other therapies such as cognitive behavioural therapy, motivational techniques, mindfulness, financial management techniques, meditation, my own experiences, social media technology, and the teachings of people such as Eckhart Tolle, Deepak Chopra, Thich Nhat Han, Daniel Kahneman, Sadhguru, Viktor E. Frankl, M. Scott Peck, and others. It takes what I deem to be the best aspects of the many therapies and theories, and incorporate them into the thirty-day recovery programme. It is important to note also that you have the *choice* of adopting whatever techniques work for you. It is not a prescriptive approach, and although it is structured and operates within a framework of techniques and strategies, ultimately you decide what elements to use.

Other treatment methods include pharmacotherapy, which covers a wide range of drug treatments such as anti-depressants, there is evidence that the SSRI paroxetine is efficient in the treatment of pathological gambling, mood stabilisers, and opioid receptors and psychodynamic/psychoanalytical approaches. I believe there is a lot of merit in these approaches. My own belief is that many gamblers do have comorbid conditions that can be addressed by these therapeutic approaches after the thirty-day recovery programme. It may be beneficial to use these therapies in conjunction with the programme, but for now the emphasis is not to include them in the thirty-day recovery programme.

1.6 Home truths about gambling

Gamblers commonly are impulsive and have urges to control events and situations. You may feel sceptical of my book, with that inner voice telling you, "I do not have a problem and will win big soon," this is the rock you will continue to perish on. Reading the previous sentence will probably compel you to prove me wrong. I am not here to compete. You have already lost; the time you spent betting uncontrollably is lost and can never be redeemed. Yes, money can be recovered, but not time. However, you can start from now to fully enjoy and immerse yourself in the time you have left on this earth. Your redemption and road to recovery will uncover untold talents and interests, interesting people, and interesting experiences. I am going to show you how, but you need to want it with all your being. Today, set the intention that "I will never gamble again" and begin the process of recovery and discovery.

In his book *Thinking, Fast and Slow*, Daniel Kahneman refers to people's predilection for trying to find causes in random events. He states, "We are pattern seekers, believers in a coherent world, in which regularities appear not by accident but as a result of mechanical causality or of someone's intention. This widespread misunderstanding of randomness sometimes has significant consequences." In the case of gamblers, this misunderstanding can be catastrophic. Rolf Dobelli refers to, in his book *the art of thinking clearly*, the *clustering illusion*; where the brain seeks patterns and rules, and if it finds no familiar patterns, it simply invents one. Many gamblers develop erroneous, false beliefs around gambling and lose all semblance of rationality when gambling. That in some way they can predict the outcome of a horse race with unerring and infallible accuracy; that they have a lucky number that the roulette ball will land on when the chips are down, that if the ball falls into the red slot three times, the next has to be black; that when they have sustained a sequence of heavy losses, a change of luck is due shortly; that a lucky charm they take with them to gambling venues has power; that they can read the mind of a fellow poker player; or that they have a psychic sense that will allow them predict the results of gambling events—all these beliefs provide *the illusion of control and power.*

I will state now that these beliefs are utter nonsense. Yes, there are mathematical permutations that can be applied to some gambling events, but bookmakers have an army of statisticians to ensure they win more than you. You may deem that you have the knack of picking winners, that extra bit of knowledge nobody else has. I put it to you then: why are bookmakers flourishing if all gamblers are so good? Why are you reading this book? These false beliefs only serve to maintain your gambling addiction. For the thirty days of this programme, I implore you to put aside all such beliefs and illogicality and to apply all your efforts in following this recovery programme. I have elaborated in more detail about common myths people have about gambling in the next section of this book (1.7 Gambling Myths).

Many people argue that gambling is an emotional and not a financial problem, which may well be true, but at this juncture in your life, it feels that financial stress is causing you the most pain and hardship. The only route, you believe, to relieving that stress is to try to recover losses incurred by taking more risk and to try to win the money owed by gambling more. But the cause of your financial problems—gambling—will not solve your financial problems. Phase three of the recovery programme, "Functioning and Economy," deals more comprehensively with financial issues, but for now, discard the notion of trying to win back money. All creditors will shout, but sometimes those who shout loudest need it the least. Let the financial chaos reign for now, and let the creditors shout for their money until you stabilise your situation, which you will achieve by working through the phases of this recovery programme.

Gambling wins generate a temporary high, but that is all. There is fundamentally no joy in winning at gambling. The thrill of a horse winning, a number coming up on roulette or a good hand in poker are all false highs, and can turn to deflating and esteem-draining lows just as easily. Real, lasting joy can only come from working at being a better person and from effort expended in personal development, not a temporary and illusory sense of joy generated by gambling wins. Testing and extending the boundaries of one's physical and mental capabilities will give great satisfaction and joy, joy that is well earned and will last.

In his book *Easy Way to Stop Smoking*, Allen Carr states that "Cigarettes do not fill a void. They create it." The exact same can be said of gambling; when not gambling, all you think about is the next bet, the next opportunity to go online or go to the bookmakers. The rest of life is not pushed aside just when you are gambling but also when you are not gambling, even when you are apparently engrossed in an activity like a work project, college assignment, socialising with friends, or watching TV. Your mind is tugged away from the present moment and into the realms of the gambling world. So any argument put forward that a gaping void will exist if you give up gambling is completely spurious; in fact, by giving up gambling, the void is removed, and you can now fully participate in life and all it has to offer.

Gambling may hide (indeed, be a causal factor in) one or many comorbid conditions such as depression, bipolar disorder, mood swings, personality disorder, anger issues, and other emotional and mental conditions. A gambling addict may have other addictions such as alcohol or substance abuse; some studies suggest that number could be up to 30 percent. A proportion of alcoholics have coexisting gambling problems, and similar proportions of gamblers suffer from alcohol dependency. It is extremely important to address these issues in tandem with or after the gambling recovery programme. Like an onion, the layers of our true selves peel away as we work through the recovery programme, and it is imperative that we deal in the best manner possible with each issue or problem as it arises.

To take on the gambling industry is not my intention. However, I would like to see a debate on gambling and how it is normalised and detoxified by the marketing approaches of the betting conglomerates, yet there are no adequate safety mechanisms in place to help those who become seriously addicted to gambling. I would welcome also accurate studies on the percentage of problem and pathological gamblers in the general populace, which I daresay is a lot higher than those figures—around 1 percent—currently trumpeted by the betting industry. This low figure can be attributed to the fact that there is no clear consensus on what defines a problem gambler, and this ambiguity means that these studies, while including all pathological gamblers, may not include all problem gamblers. Also, the greatest level of harm from gambling may come from those who are in the low to moderate risk groups by virtue of fact that these groups greatly outnumber those who are at highest risk, that is, problem and pathological gamblers.

Gambling companies are out to make a profit. They are companies and that is their right; adults are legally entitled to gamble and that is their right. But many people suffer from the effects of gambling, and comprehensive and adequate recovery and rehabilitation programmes must be put in place to ensure that the damage is mitigated and that problem and pathological gamblers can be helped out of their addiction and towards full recovery. The pervasiveness and easy accessibility of gambling channels like the Internet, phones, mobile applications, casinos, bookmaker shops, racetracks, and poker schools make it almost impossible to avoid. Almost every discussion around a sporting event must include odds on the outcome, and talk of gambling weaves its way into almost every discourse between sporting pundits.

The fastest-growing form of gambling in the world is online gambling, according to the American Gaming Association (AGA). There are over three thousand Internet gambling sites that offer betting on sports, casino games, poker, bingo, lottery, and other games. According to "Analysing the Global Online Gambling Report" (2013), "The global online gambling industry is one of the biggest and most rapidly expanding market at the moment. With a net worth of $30 billion, last year (2012) it expanded at the rate of 2.5% after a slowdown in the 2009 global economic recession and is expected to continue to grow in the coming five years." There are serious risks associated with online gambling, namely that it is easily accessed, it is especially attractive to those predisposed to develop gambling problems, the speed of games and the social isolation of online gambling may promote excessive gambling, and there is difficulty in promoting and encouraging responsible gaming amongst online gamblers.

Global gambling revenues, which includes lotteries, sports betting, online betting, and land-based casinos, climbed to more than $450 billion in 2014 and are predicted to reach $525 billion by 2019, according to the tenth edition of Global Gambling Report.

Studies have suggested that gambling is a significant contributory factor to suicide, attempted suicide and suicidal thoughts. In the United States, a report by the National Council on Problem Gambling showed approximately one in five pathological gamblers attempts suicide. The Council also said suicide rates amongst pathological gamblers are higher than for any other addictive disorder. It is of critical importance to seek medical or professional help if you are feeling suicidal. I highly recommend that you stop using alcohol, drugs, or other mind-altering substances if you are feeling extremely low or have suicidal tendencies. Consult with a family member, friend, or work colleague immediately and ask this person to accompany you to a professional medic or psychiatrist. You may feel at wit's end now, that you are a burden on other people, that you are isolated and alone, and that there is no hope, *but there is hope. You will find a way out of this dark place, and life will improve for you. Support is at hand; just reach out for it*.

Leaving monetary loss or gain aside, just think of the pointless, wasted hours spent gambling. Not only gambling itself but time spent anticipating or preparing for the gambling event, time spent concocting stories and lies to facilitate your gambling, time wasted locked away in your room totally depressed for having lost your salary that day, time wasted talking inanely to friends about your gambling exploits—the list is endless. As you emerge from your gambling addiction, you will see the value of time and that the time lost gambling was a much greater loss than any amount of money. While you cannot redeem those lost days, weeks, or years, you can maximise your time now. *Please do not waste any more time gambling. Set yourself free and enjoy the gift of life.*

1.7 Gambling myths

Many gambling addicts and problem gamblers have false beliefs and myths about gambling that only serves to maintain and sustain their gambling, in spite of heavy losses, over a protracted period of time. I have outlined below some of the common myths that many problem gamblers believe in.

Myth 1: That in some way you can influence or predict the outcome of an event.
Truth: Independent events have an equal opportunity of occurring and are totally random. The tendency to believe that we can influence something that we have no sway is called the *"illusion of control"*. Gamblers systematically over-estimate their ability to predict the outcome of events. They also incorrectly assume that near wins indicate a win is due shortly. You might as well be beaten by a mile than a nose.

Recall the times that you thought you could predict an outcome of an event such as a roulette ball landing on a certain number or colour and it did not. Dismiss this notion completely and every time you think you can influence or predict accurately the outcome of an event, repeat, either out loud or in your mind, "That an outcome of an event/wager is completely random and independent of other wagers. I cannot control or predict gambling outcomes. Period".

Myth 2: Your skill and expertise as a gambler is a reason for continuing to gamble.
Truth: The outcomes of gambling events are random and pure chance. Past outcomes are not a predictor of future outcomes. With independent events, there is no counterbalancing or harmonising effect. Those who believe there is a harmonising effect for independent events suffer from the *"gambler's fallacy"*. A lotto ball does not remember the last time it was drawn, a dice does not magically know the last number thrown or a roulette ball does not recall the last time it landed on black and so on. Also, ask yourself one question "Are you the skilled gambler who has nothing but debt, pain, and stress in your life?" I shall say no more.

Myth 3: Gambling alleviates me of boredom.
Truth: Gambling addiction creates a vacuum in your life and does not fill it. Have you ever thought of the pointless hours gambling online, in bookmakers, in a casino, at the racetrack, and so on? How you could spend hours upon hours pointlessly watching a ball roll around a roulette wheel or made your neck ache by looking at a screen watching horses running around a racetrack? How you spent hours upon hours at a poker table? What a waste of time. There is so much you could do, other than spending time unproductively gambling. Start today, get a jog in, learn some DIY skills, read that book, write that book, go for hike in the mountains, go to the museum, go and meet an old friend for a coffee, go for a swim, go for a cycle, go camping with your son or friend. I could go on forever. But if you think gambling alleviates boredom then you are gravely mistaken. Gambling is an expensive and usually foolish pastime. The gambling environment, nurtured and created by gambling companies and institutions,

only serves to create the illusion that they are fun and psychologically rewarding places to be, and this presents a false sense of comfort and security. They may seem like fun places to be, but if you are a gambling addict then they are more like a jail where you, if you continue to gamble, are building your own prison cell.

Myth 4: I have won big before so why should I not win again?

Gamblers, in the main, have selective memories and usually recall the times he or she won big. However, there were as many, if not more, times that he or she lost heavily but that episode was conveniently forgotten about. Gambling addicts are in the throes and grasp of an addiction that requires money to fuel and maintain it. Bookmakers use the harmless term "recycling of losses" to describe how punters lose all they have won on previous bets, plus a lot more, of their own hard earned cash. It does not matter if you win big, once you are a gambling addict you will always, as the bookmakers euphemistically say, "recycle" your winnings.

We treat money that we win with much less care and consideration than money that was hard earned. Richard Thaler, an American economist, calls this the *"house-money effect"*. Have you ever won large sums of money and after losing it again you say "Ah sure it was not my money to begin with; as had won it earlier". This is flawed thinking and very prevalent with gambling addicts. The money won has equal value as that money that you work hard for. Gambling companies use this effect to offer free bets to get you to register with them. You will almost certainly give it back with interest or should I say "recycle" your winnings.

Myth 5: Since I feel lucky then why should I not gamble?

Feeling lucky is exactly that, a feeling and nothing else. Feeling lucky does not make it so. The probability and chance of an event happening is the same irrespective if you feel lucky or otherwise. Remember all the times you felt lucky and lost. Gambling addicts tend to reason with emotion rather than with clear methodical mental reasoning, which can lead to grave errors in decision-making. The idea that feeling lucky will result in you winning money is completely false, dangerous, and illogical.

Myth 6: Gambling is the only option for me to address the massive debt I have accumulated.

So you are rationalising that the cause of your debt, gambling, will also be the solution. This reasoning is totally erroneous, illogical, and highly dangerous.

Irrespective of amount of debt owed, the only way to halt the decline in your financial situation is to STOP gambling. Once you stop, you will stop haemorrhaging money. Yes, it may be enticing to think that one big win will resolve all your issues, but forget that notion entirely. You have won before and have given it all back with interest, so stop that false thinking now. Your debts may seem unmanageable now, but once you stop gambling, gain some composure, and start addressing your financial situation, matters will improve. It may take months, years, decades or the rest of your life to pay off all your debt. So be it.

Myth 7: I will never be able to control my urges to gamble

Truth: Gambling urges have been conditioned and reinforced from years of gambling. Do you expect that all of a sudden the urges will go and you will feel in control? No, if course not. It took a long time for you to realise you had a severe gambling addiction. In the same vein, it will take some time for you to completely quell the urges to gamble, but for now deal with urges on a second by second, minute by minute, hour by hour, day by day basis. Follow the urge-suppression techniques in phase one "Stability" of the recovery programme, for help here. It will take time to get to a state where urges will not affect you as they do now, but step by step you will get to that place where urges will no longer affect you. It will help, in conjunction with the urge-suppression exercise, to visualise a day when you have no gambling urges, where life will no longer be pre-occupied by gambling, and where you will be able to better manage your emotions, finances, and relationships. Every day without a bet will eventually lead you to that place.

1.8 Am I a pathological or problem gambler?

There are many diagnostic criteria used to determine if you have a gambling problem. Gamblers Anonymous has a twenty-question questionnaire, and the American Psychiatric Association uses the Diagnostic and Statistical Manual (DSM) of Mental Disorders to determine whether someone meets the criteria for problem or pathological gambling, now referred to in DSM V as Disordered Gambling and classed under same category as drug and alcohol addiction. This DSM reclassification has been influenced by research that supports the position that pathological gambling and substance-use disorders are very similar in the way they affect the brain and neurological reward system. Please feel free to reference them yourself. Some of these criteria include:

- Borrowing money to finance your gambling.
- Deceiving others to hide gambling behaviours or consequences of gambling.
- Getting restless or irritable when attempting to stop gambling.
- Continued gambling despite losses and "chasing of losses."
- Risking significant opportunities (e.g., relationships and career) as a result of gambling.
- Preoccupation with gambling.
- Repeated unsuccessful attempts to control or stop gambling.

My own belief is that if you are reading this and you gamble, then you have a problem with gambling and would like help. This may be an erroneous assumption and open to contradiction. My own definition of problem gambling would go something like:

"Your life revolves around gambling activities and your gambling gains priority over your relationships, work, social activities, mental, emotional, and physical health. You invariably deny this is the case, and you are not being true to yourself and others about the effect your gambling has on you and others."

My definition has been informed by my own experiences. Every day during my addiction, the first thoughts I had in waking were invariably: "What races are on today?" "Wonder if any of my fancies will be a good price?" "How will I work around to ensure I get enough time to place my bets?" Oscar Wilde said, "Work is the curse of the drinking class." Well, you can easily replace "drinking" with the word "gambling," and it will also hold true. To extend that further, you could replace the word "work" with many others like "relationships," "meetings," or any non-gambling activity. Gambling became a total preoccupation; days melted into weeks and weeks into months.

The only timetable I ever worked towards was that dictated to me by the times of race meetings, and the opening and closing hours of casinos and bookmakers. It was a haze of pure mayhem and chaos trying to balance work, relationships, sports (which were a relief and escape when I did play), personal commitments, dealing with creditors, and so on. The most frightening aspect was how I managed to hide most of my gambling from girlfriends, friends, and colleagues. It truly amazed me how deceitful I had become. I regard myself as a very honest person, most gamblers I know are extremely honest and genuine, but the depths and lengths I would go to in order to feed or hide all traces of gambling surpassed anything I thought possible. The innumerable excuses such as how the salary payment was delayed this month, the "unforeseen payment" on the car that I had to make, the short-term cash flow issues that the loan I was seeking would sort out—it was never-ending, and every time I had to concoct more lies to help feed my addiction, it gnawed away at every fibre of my being. Lies take you away from life; truth takes you back.

For many, as gambling becomes more and more destructive and the turmoil becomes more pronounced, you target anger against yourself and others. Does gambling stoke up the embers of latent anger to a flaming inferno? Or does the gambling affliction itself make a gambler resentful and angry? Stories of gamblers inflicting pain on themselves to appease the latent anger are common. I ask myself what causes the anger in the first place. Is it guilt, fear or shame? Is it self-loathing? Is it resistance or rebellion against your situation in life? Regardless, gambling makes it worse; it is the wind that fans the flames. But once you stop gambling, you can deal with other emotions and feelings later on in recovery. One step at a time.

Gambling plays havoc with your thoughts and behaviours, routine activities become major distractions, and anything that detracts from your gambling becomes an annoyance. Everything is reprioritised: meetings with friends are cancelled, career is no longer important, holidays are put on the long finger, family activities are postponed, social and sporting activities are ignored completely. The gambler wraps himself or herself in a cocoon that is devoid of all emotion, feeling, or concern for anyone else. The less exposure he or she has to the "real world," the more time he or she has in the fantasy world of gambling, where there is no joy, just pain, suffering, devastation, and turmoil. The gambler is continuously on edge, restless, and irritable, all symptoms of a deeper emotional malaise that is deteriorating daily as the gambling persists. It feels as if every emotion, feeling, and thought is twisted into a knot of pain, your mind whirring so fast that you feel like, as The Verve sang, "I'm a million different people from one day to the next." You become desperate, and you feel totally isolated, helpless, and lost. If you are still reading and you know this is what you are going through, then go to phase one "Stability" of the recovery programme. Start there, take it one day at a time, and regain the life you have given over to gambling.

1.9 Types of gamblers

Some researchers have tried to break down problem gamblers into two distinct types based on personality traits, namely:

- Action gamblers: Assertive, confident, domineering and primarily male. Action gamblers gamble primarily at "skill" games such as poker or other card games, dice games, horse and dog racing, and sports betting. They gamble to beat other individuals or the "house" and often believe they can develop a system to achieve this goal. They appear to demonstrate reckless disregard for their losses.
- Escape or relief gamblers: Most Escape gamblers have been nurturing, caring responsible people for most of their lives. They usually gamble to escape from an underlying condition such as depression, anxiety, or emotional and psychological pain. They primarily gamble for distraction rather than for show or to enhance their reputation. Women are more likely to be relief gamblers.

It is extremely difficult to accurately categorise the type of problem gamblers, as many problem gamblers exhibit traits and behaviours that are associated with both action and escape gamblers, however, the broad categorisation helps to draw some distinction.

My own gambling, in the main, was on the horses, greyhounds, virtual racing, scratch cards, lotto, and sports events like football and boxing, with forays into the casino in the latter years of my gambling addiction. With the explosion and 24/7 access to online gambling and capability to bet on virtually any sporting event across the globe, the need to gamble is easily satisfied by logging onto your betting account via your laptop, PC, or mobile phone application. In the course of writing this guide, I have heard and read stories of gamblers who have gambled on a broad spectrum of gambling mediums including lotto, scratch cards, bookmakers, casinos, online bookmakers, and bingo. I have combined some aspects of all their stories into the anecdotes below, which, it is hoped, will show how pernicious, insidious, and damaging any form of excess gambling can be.

1.9.1 Tom's story: online gambler

Tom was enticed by the "Free €20 bet" that the online bookmaker was offering. Just download the betting application onto his iPhone, register, and presto: twenty euros to bet with. This sounded too good to be true, and it took a few years to fully realise how accurate his initial thoughts were. In the early days, Tom had some successes when betting online. Tom's acumen in predicting football scores served him well in the early days of his online betting journey and he won over €1,300 in the first four weeks of betting online. He felt confident and upped the value of his bets. Over the next six months, Tom owed over €5,000 on his credit card and had borrowed over €5,000 from his bank, under the pretence of refurbishing his house. Tom also borrowed over €4,000 from friends and family to support his online gambling. This was outside the amount he lost from his salary. In over six months, Tom had lost over €23,000. How could a free €20 bet lead to this crazy situation?

Tom began to feel the strain. He spent more and more time online, to the detriment of his relationship with his girlfriend, his work commitments, and social life. Online gambling according to Tom "was the ultimate form of escapism from his troubles," in that there was no one else to deal with while he gambled, just him and the computer or smartphone. He would be "in the zone" every time he went online, the zone of freedom where his only concern was gambling. Tom progressed to playing poker and slots online, so he literally had 24/7 window to bet on whatever took his fancy. Matters deteriorated very quickly, and the €23,000 debt spiralled to €65,000 in over three years. By falsifying loan applications, Tom had embezzled over €40,000 from his employer to feed his addiction; he had broken up with his girlfriend and had totally isolated himself from all his friends. His house was in the process of being repossessed due to substantial mortgage arrears. Tom was in utter despair when he decided to stop gambling and come clean.

Tom has not gambled in over six months; he has accepted the consequences of his actions, and is currently facing a court case on embezzlement and fraud charges. However, today Tom does not gamble. He has built up a solid network of friends through his attendance at GA meetings and by volunteering at a local community organisation. Tom also managed to renegotiate a split mortgage with his bank, which has allowed him to stay in his home. He is single but is concentrating on rebuilding his life. He is extremely regretful and sorry for his criminal actions in embezzling money from his former employer. He is worried, of course, about the forthcoming court case but not overly concerned about the stigma attached to it and possible conviction for fraud. Tom is expecting to get up to two years in prison if convicted, but he is realistic, magnanimous, and accepting of his situation. Tom will accept whatever sentence is handed down to him, but as he says himself, "I can only be the best person I can be today, and that is all a person can do."

1.9.2 Peter's story: scratch card and lotto addict

Peter saw the TV advertisement for the latest "Big Winner" of the National Lottery draw. The winner shared with another lucky winner, and both received over €2.5 million each—a life-changing sum. Peter daydreamed about what he would do with that sort of money: go on a world cruise, buy a new house by the sea, pay off all his debts, treat the family to a nice holiday, and pay for the best education that he could get for his children. Peter, over the course of the next year, began gambling heavy by buying National Lottery scratch cards and lotto tickets for the twice weekly National Lottery draw.

At the height of his addiction, Peter would buy over one hundred scratch cards a day. Peter was convinced that he would scratch out a big prize win, to the extent that on occasions his fingers would bleed from the amount of frenzied and manic scratching he would do. Peter mentioned how the "small wins" kept him hooked and only served to reinforce his destructive behaviour. No one suspected Peter of having a problem, and with the easy availability of scratch cards, Peter was not bound to buy a large bulk in any one shop, which may have highlighted his problem. Peter also increased the amount he bet on the twice weekly lotto draw in a desperate attempt to recoup his losses. Peter became so desperate that he pawned some family heirlooms to get money to feed his addiction. Peter also gambled money that was put aside for his children's college education. Matters came to a head when Peter's wife found a large bag of discarded scratch cards in Peter's car. Peter broke down and admitted to his addiction.

Peter immediately began on his road to recovery, accepted the consequences of his behaviours, and worked hard in rebuilding his life. Today Peter is free from gambling. He takes meticulous care to not to enter outlets where scratch cards are sold, and only brings enough cash to pay for the groceries he intends to buy. Peter's wife controls all credit and debit cards, and to help keep busy, Peter has taken up golf and undertaken a night course in addiction studies, both of which he enjoys immensely.

1.9.3 Jim's story: casino addict

Jim's first night in the casino was through a work outing. Jim felt like he was in a scene from a James Bond movie—the rattle of the ball as it coursed around the roulette wheel, the click of chips in the hands of players as they studiously glanced at the dealer who placed the cards on the green baize of the blackjack table, the free drinks that were offered by the attractive waitresses, and the salubrious surroundings of the casino floor all culminated into making it a wonderful night out. Jim decided to go to the casino again on his own, and it felt like the calm eye of the hurricane that was his work and domestic life.

Jim was having marital issues and his workload was overbearing. The casino was a welcome reprieve from the pressure cooker of his life. Jim won handsomely at roulette on his first few attempts—his lucky number had served him well—and he deemed he was a crack-shot at blackjack.

As the weeks and months passed, Jim's luck ran out. He gradually upped the ante of bets on the roulette wheel. He thought he was due a change of luck and just knew it would come soon. Jim alternated his betting between the blackjack table and the roulette wheel, on many occasions playing both at same time, jumping manically between the tables.

Jim's luck did not change, and he lost over €100,000 in ten months. Jim earned a high salary and managed to secure loans from his bank and maxed out his five credit cards. However, the debt was unsustainable and he was running to a standstill in trying to hide his debts from those closest to him. After a late night and heavy losses at the casino; Jim drove his car recklessly home. He no longer cared about his own or other people's welfare. He careered off the road and hit a ditch. Luckily, Jim only suffered minor injuries, but it left him in a state of total shock and disbelief at what he had done. He opened up about his gambling addiction to his brother; with whom he is very close. Jim stopped gambling, sought help, and worked at repairing the damage done to his marriage, career, and relationships with his close friends and family. Jim does not gamble today; he has found a new lease on life at work, is reducing his debt, has agreed on a five-year plan with all his creditors, and spends a lot more time with his family and friends.

1.9.4 Ann's story: bingo addict

Ann enjoyed the camaraderie of fellow bingo players. The bingo hall Ann frequented was open seven nights a week; she normally would attend at least three evenings most weeks but often frequented five or six nights. Ann usually babysat for her daughter on a Saturday night, so that night she never went to the local hall.

Ann played up to four or five books at a time and would play for hours on end. Her husband had died over two years previous and the bingo provided Ann with a social outlet and somewhere to go to break the tedium of the week.

However, Ann became totally preoccupied with bingo. Her every waking hour was given over to thinking about playing bingo and anticipating going to the bingo hall. Ann discovered online bingo and started playing that in the morning and during the day prior to going to the bingo hall. Ann spent her savings on feeding her bingo addiction; she even stopped babysitting for her daughter on Saturday evenings as the addiction got worse.

Ann became depressed, suffered from anxiety and panic attacks, and no longer made an effort on her personal appearance. Ann began to forego basic domestic tasks like cleaning and washing, and for a woman so house-proud, this was a shock to her friends and family. Ann started to borrow money from her sons and daughters and began to avoid friends at the bingo hall, whom she now deemed as a hindrance in her quest to win a big jackpot.

Ann's son confronted her on her destructive bingo playing. Ann succumbed and admitted how it had consumed her life. Ann attended a local Gamblers Anonymous group and her family were very supportive in her recovery. Ann began to work at a local soup kitchen and joined a local theatre group, where she is excelling in her newfound love. Ann no longer plays bingo or has any desire to, but is fully aware that she needs to keep on her guard.

CHAPTER 2
Programme Introduction

2.1 Introduction

The 30 + 1 Day Recovery Programme is a thirty-day programme that equips recovering problem gamblers with techniques to deal with gambling urges and the financial, emotional, legal, and relational difficulties caused by their gambling behaviour. The "+ 1" refers to each single day of the rest of the recovering problem gambler's life after the thirty-day programme. The recovery programme is geared to all types and profile of gamblers such as online gamblers, bingo players, poker players, gamblers who gamble in bookies or at racing tracks, scratch card addicts and lotto players. I have created a website called www.how-to-stop-gambling.com; this will act as resource and complement to this book and will contain online discussion forums, copies of worksheets used in this programme, videos, blogs, and more.

I wanted to incorporate five important core concepts in the recovery programme that, I feel, are necessary to overcome a gambling addiction. These concepts are as follows:

- *Structure*: The recovering gambling addict lives in a chaotic world. A structured programmatic approach of recovery will help bring stability to his or her life.
- *Choice*: To dictate to recovering problem gamblers what they should and should not do is, I believe, not the right approach. I have provided a recovery programme that while based on a structured framework, is not prescriptive and allows choice

in terms of what coping strategies the recovering gambling addict chooses to adopt in his or her recovery.
- *Empathy*: The reader should feel that the writer can see things from his or her perspective. There is a bond that will strengthen as we work through the programme.
- *Objectives and timeframes*: If we do not set ourselves specific, attainable goals and have set timeframes to achieve them, then more than likely they will never be achieved. The goals also help us concentrate on the important things in life and not be distracted by unimportant things.
- *Coping strategies and techniques*: Setting goals is fine, but recovering problem gamblers need advice and guidance on how to achieve them.

I have broken down the programme into three phases and a chapter called "Pillars," which is geared to maintaining and sustaining your recovery after completion of the three phases. Each phase details the steps to be taken and the coping techniques that will accompany each phase to help you work through and reach the next phase of the recovery programme. I want to re-emphasise the point that the programme is structured in terms of phases, but you have the *choice* of which coping techniques you adopt in order to maintain and sustain your recovery.

I recommend that you start immediately and do not delay until you feel more equipped or in a better frame of mind. If you really want to stop gambling, then start the programme NOW and recover your life. It is not as if you are actually sacrificing a great hobby or interest; this is the activity that has brought you to your knees, has brought poverty to your door, and has damaged, if not destroyed, your relationships, so why would you want to delay starting the programme?

The acronym I have used for the phases of the recovery programme is SAFE. I have termed the approach the "SAFEstep™" method.

Phase 1: **S**tability

Phase 2: **A**cceptance

Phase 3: **F**unctioning and **E**conomy

The recovery programme is thirty days in duration. In reality, the programme is lifelong, but once the thirty days is reached, you will have been provided with all the basic tools and coping techniques to help you manage and sustain your recovery from gambling addiction.

Each phase of the recovery programme outlines the objectives of the phase and the coping techniques to help you get through that phase. *It is highly important that the skills you learn and coping strategies you adopt in each phase are continued into the next phase.*

The choice of which coping techniques you adopt is up to you. You may decide that you can work with one or two techniques to help you through each phase, but obviously the more techniques you adopt the better chance you have of progressing. It is vital that you read through the chapter for each phase every day of the recovery programme. The objective here is for you to accumulate more and more coping skills that will enable you reach the end of the programme, and to continue using those skills to sustain you on your road to full recovery and a normal, happy, and bet-free life. Avoid the temptation to read on to the next phase; rather, concentrate wholeheartedly on each phase for the duration of time allocated to that phase of recovery. During each day of each phase of the recovery programme, take time to imagine life free of the shackles of gambling—no more running around heedlessly trying to cover your tracks, no more lies, no more irritability or mood swings, no more time wasted, and more time to devote to your family, friends, hobbies, and interests.

I want to emphasise that I do not agree with "controlled gambling," where you reduce the amount spent on gambling or the frequency of gambling, but there is a middle ground that may be suitable for some gamblers. That will be elaborated on in phase one of the programme ("Stability").

During the course of your recovery, always hold your head high and act in a dignified and responsible manner. Although you may have done things that you are ashamed of, that was a result of being in the stranglehold of a condition that is not easy to overcome. Be compassionate and be easy on yourself; do not beat yourself up over past failings, indiscretions, or illegal acts committed to fuel your gambling addiction. Be compassionate with yourself when you find the recovery tough going; you will face tough days, but you are making a recovery, and each day without a bet is a good day. Yes, you will face obstacles, challenges, and sometimes loneliness along the way, but a better life awaits you. Be strong, have faith in yourself, and recover that great person you left behind when you started gambling.

CHAPTER 3
Phase One: STABILITY

3.1 Introduction

Duration: Ten days (day one to day ten)

On successful completion of phase one of the "SAFEstep™" method, "Stability", it is important to reward yourself. This can be a meal out with your spouse or partner, treat yourself to a new item of clothes, meet a friend for a coffee, an overnight stay in the country, go bowling with friends, go to the movies, and so on. While finances may be very tight, allocate some budget and/or time for this reward. Agree this with a partner, spouse, family member, or friend.

3.2 Phase one goals and objectives

- Stop gambling for ten consecutive days.
- Achieve some normality and structure in day-to-day living; where your focus is a bit clearer, allowing you to enter phase two of the recovery programme.
- Strengthen your emotional resolve and willpower to deal with the wave of gambling urges that will continue to assault your senses; however, these urges will abate over time.

3.3 Phase one overview

Phase one, "Stability", covers two areas, namely "STOP" and "Structure" that are critical in ensuring you overcome the initial gambling urges that you will inevitably experience.

The first phase of not gambling is simply **STOP** placing bets.

STOP. Make the choice. Every decision you have made in your life, even to start gambling, was a choice. Everything in life is a choice. How you choose to react to events, people, and situations and how you react to thoughts, compulsions, desires, and emotions are all choices you make. However, you can choose to react differently, and that is the key to recovery. To bet on a race, roulette wheel, online casino game, poker, or sporting event entails a choice; you can decide to bet on it or not. This may sound simple, but when you are in the throes of an out-of-control gambling addiction, it may seem impossible or unrealistic. Nevertheless, it is true. So to start this recovery process, you need to stop placing bets, be it betting online, betting through bookies, buying scratch cards, playing poker, or buying any form of raffle tickets.

I will not lie; this will be overwhelmingly difficult for many reasons: you have hardwired and conditioned your thought and behavioural patterns around gambling, and you have always placated and satisfied your urges generated by these patterns by placing bets. You will have seemingly insurmountable debt and feel that the only way to pay it back is through further gambling to see if you can recover losses incurred. You may have to deal with a relationship breakdown as a result of your gambling. You may feel very vulnerable being removed from the camaraderie and company of fellow gamblers and the false comfort zone and security of a betting establishment, casino, or online betting room. You may feel totally restless and unable to sit still, but that is also normal behaviour at this stage. However, the overriding objective is to not place a bet. To help here, I have listed a range of coping techniques to help you through phase one. Rest assured that any loss of face or credibility for undertaking some of these steps will be nothing compared to the massive benefits you will gain from gambling recovery.

You may think that stopping gambling will not rid you of your financial despair or repair the damage done to your relationships, and that the immediate pressure is unbearable. That may sound true right now, but it is not the case. For phase one your total focus should be on stopping gambling and the basic subsistence of food and sleep is all that is needed. Phases two and three will help you deal with the associated problems caused by gambling.

This phase, "Stability," also includes "Structure". This basically refers to putting some shape and form to your day. Gambling will have preoccupied you and consumed most of your time over the last few years or decades. Stopping gambling will temporarily create a vacuum in your life and as the old saying states "nature abhors a vacuum." It is highly important you have a daily schedule that will occupy your time. Work on a daily schedule for the each day of the programme; put together a daily schedule the evening before, for example, schedule time slots for work, lunch, walking, rest periods, gym, library, meeting a friend, and so on, and stick to the schedule as best you can.

This phase will also include urge-suppression techniques that you can use anytime during the course of the programme and beyond.

3.4 Coping techniques for phase one "Stability"

Be aware you can use one, some, or all of the options here depending on how great your compulsion is (it will vary from day to day). I have listed those coping techniques that are most vital; there is free choice here in what techniques you adopt, but the stronger the gambling urge, the more techniques you will need to employ.

3.4.1 Recommended coping techniques

- Attend Gamblers Anonymous meetings. I would recommend you attend meetings for at least the first ten days of your stopping gambling. I earlier elaborated on my views of the GA approach, but for now, attend as many meetings as possible. This will allow you share your pain with like-minded souls, give you some structure to your day, and help get you through phase one. For now, do not feel obligated to follow the GA twelve-step programme; just be in the presence of recovering problem gamblers and talk about your pain openly at meetings. You can decide later on in recovery whether the twelve-step programme is something you would like to follow.
- Take a piece of paper and list on left side column the benefits of continuing to gamble and on the right hand column, list the benefits of not gambling. Your emotional reaction to anything determines how you assess the benefits and risks. So in the case of gambling, you will deem the risks smaller and the benefits greater. Gamblers have a tendency only to think of the positive consequences of gambling; the times they have won money and overlook the times they lost entire pay packets. However, that is selective thinking and incorrect. Let me remind you that the fact that you are currently in debt indicates you have lost far more than you have won. In doing this exercise, think of all the times you cancelled dates, avoided meeting with family or friends, holidays with partner or friends you had to forego, the hours lost watching a horse running around a track or a ball spinning around a roulette wheel, the career you sacrificed, the hardship you caused those closest to you, the cherished memories of seeing your children growing up that you missed out on, the lying and deceit you perpetuated to sustain your gambling, potential imprisonment as a result of a crime you may have committed to fund your gambling, impact on your

health, and the debt levels you currently have. Think also of the benefits of not gambling such as improved finances, better sleep, better health, more time to spend with your partner, family and friends, more positive outlook on life, development of new or existing friendships, less stress and anxiety, and so on. The benefit analysis sheet (Appendix 5) can be used here.
- Hand over all credit cards, debit cards, and excess cash to a trusted friend, confidante, or family member, and keep enough money for food and basic items such as car fuel, phone, bus fares, and so on. Your trusted confidante will provide you the necessary funds each day to just cover these basic costs. Some people may not be able to confide in somebody or know somebody to entrust their credit cards with. In this case, it might be best to destroy all credit and debit cards and budget meticulously for each day with the available cash you have. Again, you have a choice here: if you feel you can manage credit cards and cash, then that is fine. These are suggested techniques and not orders. In most cases these are temporary measures until you regain emotional, mental, and financial stability. Money and credit, your gambling capital, are the fuel that drives your gambling addiction, so it is important to minimise access to money and credit other than for core living expenses.
- Avoid all contact with betting establishments, associates who gamble, talk of gambling, online gambling websites, racing on TV, and newspapers (sporting editions and designated sporting press). If you inadvertently meet a gambler or have cause to discuss gambling, then make your excuses and move on. Some gamblers exclude themselves from bookmakers, local casinos, and so on. However, with the omnipresent 24/7 access to online gambling, this measure may only be effective in some cases. Another option would be to block all gambling websites on your browser using a net blocker like GamBlock.

- Close down ALL your online betting accounts.
- Work on a daily schedule for the next day; do this the evening before, for example, schedule time slots for work, lunch, walking, rest periods, gym, library, meeting a friend, and so on, and stick to the schedule as best you can. Try and do this each evening for the entire thirty-day programme. Make sure to do a schedule for just the next day and not a weekly planner—just day by day. I have kept it simple; there is no need to have rigid times for events, but set yourself tasks and exercises that need to be completed in the morning, afternoon, and evening. Do not pressure yourself to do all tasks; the key is to keep busy and keep your mind occupied. Try changing or varying some of the activities you day each day. See the daily diary template and example in appendix 1. The daily diary template can be downloaded from *www.how-to-stop-gambling.com*
- Recall your last bet and how utterly awful you felt; write down the feelings, the pain, the emotional trauma, and the anguish. Write it down on paper, in a word-processing document, or in a text message; this will be there to remind you whenever you think of gambling again and why you can never go back to that dark place.
- Be compassionate with yourself; do not criticise yourself or others. Imagine a mature, caring, considerate, compassionate, warm, forgiving, and non-judgmental self offering a helping hand and lending a sympathetic ear during the difficult days of your recovery.
- You will probably feel that the world has imploded in on you, extraordinarily stressed, and that your emotional and financial states are too difficult to bear. You may imagine all the worst-case scenarios. Financial pressure, in particular, may be unbearable (but you will resolve this in time). Please put all these concerns aside for now, no matter how difficult that may be; we will deal in a rational and prudent way with emotional,

PHASE ONE: STABILITY

financial, legal, and other issues in later phases of recovery. Most pathological and problem gamblers will face these issues, and by taking one step at a time, no matter how serious it seems now, you will address and resolve these issues. But for now, just put all your efforts into *not gambling*. You will recover, be patient, be strong, keep positive and things will improve, slowly maybe, but they will improve.

- You may be under severe pressure or have received physical threats to repay a loan from a money lender, loan shark or other third party (possibly underworld figures). The recommendation is to talk directly with them and propose a repayment schedule. However, I would suggest, you do talk with creditors only when you are in a better frame of mind, so delay in talking with creditors as long as you deem necessary. Ensure you can meet this repayment schedule. If this is not accepted then, as last resort, consider getting a loan from family or close friend (and explain the circumstances). If a threat is made against you, your family or property, report it to the police immediately.
- If betting urges are over-bearing, then occupy yourself with anything that requires your mental focus and will occupy you until the urge abates. A useful technique is to first close your eyes, second, take a deep breath by mentally counting to 4 as you inhale, expanding your stomach as you do so, then hold your breath for another 4 seconds, before exhaling deeply, feel all your worries flow out with each exhalation of breath, do this until you feel calmer. When you are calmer try to test your memory or put focus on anything at all that will occupy your mind for the next while. Examples here include: listing mentally or on a piece of paper all classmates you had in school or college, list the TV programmes you liked as a kid, do a crossword, write an email to a close friend, learn the lyrics of a song, do

an intense physical workout for a few minutes, think of or recall some jokes you can use at the next party you go to, walk to the shops, read a few paragraphs of a book, paint, do some DIY around the house, cook a meal and so on. Be prepared and have a list of options of things to do when the urges come upon you, keep this list on your person if you need to. Comprehensive urge-suppression techniques are outlined in more detail in section 3.5 of this chapter.
- Write down three things in life that are most precious to you and that you are most grateful for, and keep this on your person. Recall or take them out and look at them when urges to gamble are strong. Tell yourself, "If I gamble, I will lose or damage the three most important things in my life."
- On cessation of gambling, you may encounter some of the following symptoms such as sleeplessness, irritability, remorse, regret, lack of concentration, anxiety, sense of emptiness, depression, low mood, and have obsessive thoughts. These symptoms are normal and view them as part of your recovery. However, observe these feelings, images, memories, and thoughts and let them be, they will slowly subside and go. If you feel overwhelmed with thoughts of suicide, self-harm or harm to others, then consult a counsellor, doctor or medical professional.
- Read through phase one, "Stability", chapter of this book every day, as many times as you like, the more the better. Avoid reading about the other phases; just concentrate on phase one.

3.4.2 Suggested coping techniques

- If possible, undertake some physical exercise: brisk walk, jog, gym work out, cycle, swim, hike, or some other activity that involves physical exertion. This will allow you temporary distraction from urges and temporary reprieve from your problems. Not only will physical activity help preoccupy your mind and take it off gambling, it will also release brain chemicals (endorphins) and improves the action of neurotransmitters such as serotonin, noradrenaline and dopamine that will improve your mood and make you feel better. Physical activity will also boost your endurance and energy, which is vital to counteract the lethargy that may accompany you on your journey of recovery. Also, sleep may be improved by exercising more. Exercise, like walking in the forest, hiking, mountaineering, and so on can be beneficial from a physical, spiritual and emotional level. Thirty minutes of exercise a day should be a general goal. Slowly build up your fitness and set yourself realistic goals; for example, walk one mile a day for the first week, two miles in the second week, and so on. Ensure to warm-up and stretch before you exercise, and stretch and warm-down after.

- You may be under intense pressure from creditors, family, or friends who lent you money. Let them know you will contact them within the next three weeks after you do something highly important. There is no need to let anyone know immediately, except for a close confidante, a partner, or GA members what your predicament is. As you work through the programme, we will deal with these issues one by one. It is highly critical that you are not distracted from your efforts to *not gamble*.
- Meet with a close friend, family relative or counsellor with whom you can talk openly and honestly. If GA or counselling is not an option, then it is important to talk with someone who can compassionately and empathetically listen to you without judgment. Try to meet this person for at least one hour a day for the first five days. If you do not have someone to confide in, then refer to the many agencies that offer

online and telephone support; many are listed in Appendix 7 of this book.
- If needed, take some time off work, if you are employed, of course. However, work can preoccupy you and could render you better equipped to deal with the urges to gamble, so consider this option carefully. You might consider taking a day or two off at the start of phase one.
- For each day of the thirty-day programme, sit comfortably for five minutes (longer if you can); envision a life without gambling, the time spent with loved ones, time spent doing productive healthy pursuits, wholesome sleep, no financial woes, travel, holidays, and normal working and personal relationships. Imagine a day with no stress, no running around manically to get a bet on, no phone calls from people looking for money, no letters from banks threatening legal action, no more lies to a loved one, no more anxiety and panic, no more churning in the pit of your stomach as you wantonly squander another large sum of cash. Write this down and keep it on your person if you want to. This will come to you one day, but every time you feel the urge to gamble during phase one, take a seat, take a few deep breaths, and replay this image in your mind, focus on this image, and know that overcoming these urges will lead you to that life. Make the choice; you now have control over what life you want to lead and live. You now have the power to dictate the outcome of events, which was never the case with your gambling. Deal with urges minute by minute, second by second, and keep calm and focus on what life will be like when you are free of the gambling addiction. Observe the urges, the emotions, images, memories, and thoughts they generate, but do not act on them; just observe them and let them slowly subside and fade away. By accepting and just observing the thought, you will disarm the emotional reaction to the thought of gambling and quell the urge.

- Spend one to five minutes each day to sit and focus on your breath. Do not change the pattern of your breath. Let everything—your breath, your current circumstances, your painful surreal world—be exactly as it is. Observe your breath; your mind will wander, but as it does, slowly bring your focus back on your breathing. You may last one minute or five minutes doing this. Do not worry; the more you do it, the calmer your mind will become.
- Visualise making a promise to a loved one—spouse, child, parent, brother, sister—that you will not gamble again. See how happy you will make that person by never gambling again and how they will be so proud of you for overcoming a stifling and debilitating condition. Visualise also the outcome of breaking that promise, the disappointment and pain in that person's face caused by you capitulating and giving in to gambling, and how you chose gambling over them. See how not gambling will make such a positive change, not only to your life but to all whose lives you touch.
- Each day of the thirty-day programme, set the intention and repeat on rising, "I will not gamble today."

3.5 Urge Suppression Techniques

The urge to gamble will well up in you almost every minute of the day for the first few weeks of stopping gambling; however the urges will reduce in intensity over time. It is suggested that you read through the techniques below and adopt the technique(s) that suit you best. You can use these techniques any time during the recovery programme. You may find that the recommended and suggested coping strategies of this phase, listed above, are sufficient in quelling your urges. However, if urges are overwhelming then adopt one or more of the techniques outlined below.

3.5.1 Gambling process

From my own gambling behaviours, I have identified the steps and factors involved in a normal gambling engagement. There are effectively eight parts of the gambling process, namely:

- *Environmental trigger*: This can be further broken down into one or all of the following:
    - Location: entering a bookmaker's or casino, logging on to a betting website, etc.
    - Emotional state: high or low mood, feeling vulnerable, bored, and needing to preoccupy oneself by gambling.
    - Event: finding an escape from domestic issues, a relationship breakup, etc., by placing a bet.
    - Social environment: around friends, family, and colleagues who gamble.
- *Urge*: This will be caused by the environmental situation you find yourself in, where the urge to gamble can well up, compelling you with almost irresistible force to place a bet.
- *Anticipation*: Eager anticipation of engaging with the gambling medium. This may be accompanied by irritability or tension if prevented from gambling.
- *Placing a bet*: This is the actual act of placing a bet; this can be putting a chip on a roulette table, buying a scratch card, placing a bet with bookies, placing a bet online, and so on.
- *Engagement with betting medium*: This is the actual interaction with a betting medium, for example, watching a horse race, watching a roulette wheel, watching the reels in a slot machine, scratching the scratch card, looking at a lotto drawing, and so on.
- *Arousal*: Adrenaline rush as gambling activity unfolds e.g., horse race or spin of ball around roulette wheel. Total focus

on the gambling event with associated excitement and physical arousal shown by increased heart rate.
- *Post bet feeling*: For example, feeling down, angry, guilty, remorseful, worried or fearful if bet does not come in or feeling relieved, confident, elated, and ecstatic if it does.
- *Post-bet behaviours*: This is how you react after either winning or losing the bet. Do you walk away? Do you get contorted in emotional pain? Do you hurry to place another bet? It is also how you engage with and treat your partner, spouse, family, friends, and colleagues.

The total process will equal the time spent gambling. Time cannot be recovered; there are 86,400 seconds in a day. How you spend your time in that window is your choice. You can spend it happily and productively or spend it wantonly and wastefully by gambling. Time cannot be redeemed; you cannot carry forward a balance of time from the previous day.

The conditioning of the brain and the re-enforcement of neural reward pathways in the brain ensure that those pre-disposed to gambling addiction will, if continue to engage in gambling activity, in time, become gambling addicts.

The two most important aspects to manage and address are the general gambling urges and the urge to actually place a bet. I draw a distinction here between the urge to actually place a bet and a gambling urge, the latter pertains more to the actual thought of gambling or thought of going to a gambling establishment, the former is the urge to physically place a bet in a betting establishment or online.

3.5.2 Dealing with the urge to place a bet

In an analysis of the five parts of the process, the most detrimental part is the actual placing of the bet in hope of a return. The actual parting of money and how the associated monetary loss affects your mood, financial state, focus, emotions, feelings, and so on is where the real impact of gambling is—aside from the time lost, of course. This may lead to "chasing of losses" which is the betting of larger amounts than normal in a bid to recover losses, further perpetuating the cycle of losses and exacerbating the situation.

We will look at managing and dealing with the other four parts of the gambling process in more detail later. In this phase, we will look at techniques, tools, and strategies to help you repress and control the urges to gamble. In phase three, "Functioning and Economy," we will look at how to deal with the financial, relational, social, and emotional problems caused by your gambling. However, addressing first the most damaging part of the gambling process, placing a bet, is paramount. What I am proposing may run counter to all other theories of gambling addiction recovery, but from my own experience and the experience of other recovering problem gamblers I have worked with, this technique has proved successful.

There are two techniques, referred to as *imaginal exposure techniques,* that can be adopted here.

So to reiterate, these techniques deal with the part of the gambling process that is the urge to actually place a bet. I would like to note that this is a short-to-medium-term measure. The idea is to reduce dependency on these techniques over time. Some may never need to use these techniques, whereas others may need to use them for a short period of time and others for a longer period. As stated earlier, the idea is to maximise your productive time and reduce time spent on the unhealthy activity of gambling.

3.5.3 What are these techniques?

It is important to note that if any exposure to a gambling medium causes your mind to race or raises anxiety then proceed directly to section 3.5.4 "Dealing with general gambling urges." These techniques are not suitable for all gamblers, and like all techniques in this recovery programme, you have the choice of which techniques you adopt to aid your recovery.

Technique one

It might be best to use this technique later on in the recovery programme, once your emotional and mental resolve is stronger.

This technique is actually mimicking the placing of a bet but with no money being exchanged or lost; it is in effect a process of virtual betting. Why would you want to do this? Well, for a few reasons:

- To go cold turkey and not satiate the actual process of gambling that you have hardwired and conditioned your mind and body to, would be reckless in my opinion, and may lead to a relapse to "real" gambling.
- You are running with the gambling urges for now, not against them; resistance causes pain and inevitably leads to relapse. Over a period of time, as you develop and strengthen your coping techniques, the urges dissipate and consequently so does your need to use this technique.
- No further financial damage will accrue by using this technique.

The objective is to quell and suppress the urges to place a bet.

The technique here is to write out or imagine yourself placing a bet and watching the event unfold, be it a horse race, a football match, or a lotto drawing and so on. Let the event unfold; you may have predicted or not predicted the outcome, but that is immaterial. Do not assume you were wrong to stop gambling if you successfully predicted the outcome. If you feel that way, then you are missing the ultimate objective here, and that is to satisfy the urge of placing a bet. You are in effect fooling the mind, and it is not fooling you (as was the case). Again, the key here is to reduce the frequency and time spent doing this technique and to concentrate on the other coping techniques outlined in the programme. *Important also to note that this technique is NOT done in a betting establishment; it is only to be done in one's own home by watching TV or in some cases looking at an event online.*

Many may argue that this technique only continues to feed the urge and that it will only be a matter of time before the recovering problem gambler reverts back to normal gambling. However, my view is that going with the gambling urge for now, without spending money, will allow recovering problem gamblers to concentrate on developing better coping strategies in other areas of their lives, such as those outlined in phase three, "Functioning and Economy." However, as detailed previously, there is a choice, and if after a period of time this technique is used to the detriment of all other coping techniques, then the choice has to be to stop using it and concentrate more time on other coping techniques. The technique will not suit all recovering problem gamblers, but for many it may be suitable. So I am going to leave to you, the recovering problem gambler, to decide whether or not to adopt this technique.

Technique two

Another useful technique that you can use in conjunction with the relaxation technique (Section 3.5.4 "Dealing with general gambling urges") is to imagine yourself going through the betting process. *In this technique, unlike the previous technique, you DO NOT watch the gambling event unfold.* It might be best to lie down to do this technique; if you have to lie on a carpet or sofa, so be it. As the urge overcomes you, lie down, close your eyes gently, rest your legs and keep them uncrossed, rest your arms by your side, and imagine your legs and arms sinking into the mattress/floor/sofa. Now, take deep breaths into your abdomen and expand your belly and then exhale all of the air of your body, let all your worries and anxiety go with your out breath, and imagine your breath tapering off like a stream into the ceiling. Now as you relax, imagine yourself going to the bookmakers or logging on to your online betting account or going to the casino. Create a vivid picture of the surroundings, the placing of the bet, the event unfolding (horse race, roulette, playing poker, and so on), and go with the feelings the image conjures. Try and focus on your breathing as you do this. Now imagine how you will feel as you place the bet, the feelings of guilt, despair and disappointment as you place the bet, you may feel anxious but observe those feelings too. Take a few more deep breaths and relax further into the mattress or sofa. Now, imagine yourself NOT placing the bet and not giving into the urge. Feel the pride, joy, and satisfaction of not giving into the urge. Now continue to breathe gently. When you feel the urge has dissipated, open your eyes, raise yourself slowly, and feel proud for not succumbing to the urge and say "Well Done" to yourself. Now occupy yourself for the rest of the day with the many activities that you now have the time to do. If there are lesser urges during the day, simply shout "STOP!" Either vocally or in your head and let the thought of gambling fade away.

3.5.4 Dealing with general gambling urges

It is inevitable that you will have compelling urges to gamble. Your thought and behaviour patterns have been hardwired to act on these urges by gambling. It will take some time to eliminate these urges. The key here is to not act on these urges; see the urges as part of the recovery process. Each time you do not yield to an urge, you are taking a step closer to full recovery. It has been scientifically proven that if we can resist an urge for up to an hour, maybe less in many cases, then the urge will completely go. This is the basis for the technique outlined below.

An urge can be triggered by getting access to cash, a bad day at work, boredom, passing a betting office, seeing an advertisement by a gambling company, drinking alcohol (lowering inhibitions and losing control), creditors threatening you for their cash, or an argument with your partner, and so on. There are numerous triggers that can cause these gambling urges. I will outline below five steps to help you repress these urges. This will take about eight to ten minutes to complete.

Step 1: Sit down somewhere private immediately, if impractical to sit or get a private space then stay where you are, take one deep breath, breathe through your nose, and follow the breath as it enters your body, through your nostrils, down into your lungs, and deep into your belly. Then make a large exhalation through your mouth. Feel your lungs, belly, and abdomen empty, and imagine the breath trailing off into the distance like a gentle gust of wind. As you breathe in through your nostrils, expand your stomach, and as you breathe out through your mouth, deflate your stomach. Do this fifteen times. Do not mind if people stare at you; let them stare.

Step 2: Recall the memory you have of your last day gambling; if you have it saved on a piece of paper in your wallet or on your phone as a text, take it out and read it slowly. If not, recall the image mentally. Remember the pain? Remember the total desperation? Remember the chaos in your mind, the feeling of dread and despair? Also, recall the image of making a promise to a loved one that you would never gamble again, and imagine how the person would feel, look, and react if you did gamble again. Recall it, dwell on it for two minutes, and continue to observe your breath.

Step 3: Continue monitoring your normal breathing. Observe the breath entering your nostrils, into your body, and out your mouth. Feel yourself becoming calmer and calmer. Now focus on the image of life without gambling, the life without chaos, no financial woes, no lies, no deception, happy relationships, and no more madness. Dwell on this for two minutes while continuing to breathe calmly.

Step 4: Rise slowly and distract yourself for the next fifty minutes; take a walk, jog, cycle, visit your friend, watch a movie, play golf, go fishing, read a chapter of a book, do some gardening, meet or call your confidante (partner, friend, GA member) and talk it through—you decide. Ideally, it should be an activity you really enjoy. If it takes up the rest of your day, so be it; the urge to gamble has been repressed. Remember also to concentrate totally and mindfully on what you do. If it is a walk or jog, feel the movement of your body, the soles of your feet hitting the ground, the air on your face; take in the surroundings. If cooking, concentrate on each task fully, like the cutting of vegetables and the smell of the food. Immerse yourself in the experience, and try to block out all other thoughts. When you are eating, chew only your food, not your fears, angers, and concerns. Enjoy the experience of eating and put aside all other thoughts. If your mind wanders, gently bring your focus back on eating.

Step 5: After the urge has subsided, ask yourself what caused the urge. Make sure you look at this and figure out how you can avoid the triggering event in the future. For example, if passing the bookmakers triggered the urge, then avoid that route in the future. Or if you had a row with your partner, then be frank and let him or her know how the argument affected you. Or if you got paid and felt like gambling, then ideally let your confidante control your credit and debit cards until you feel ready to take back control. In appendix 3, there is a simple table you can use to record the urges—when they happened, why they happened, and how you felt. It's up to you whether you want to record them or not, you may find it useful.

3.6 Summary of phase one

It may be the case that you are being evicted from your home and repossession of your property is in progress, you are facing legal proceedings, you have been fired from work, you have committed serious fraud, or many other events are happening that may seem life-changing, in retrospect, it will not be as bad as they seem right now. You may feel totally distraught and overwhelmed by what has happened, in total panic, and you may have thoughts about self-harm or suicide. You MUST NOT act on these thoughts. People will help. Please reach out to those closest to you or to the many organisations that are listed in Appendix 7 of this book. Things will get better, no matter how bad or serious they seem now, and you will get your life back that you have given over to the gambling addiction.

Your brain state has been conditioned and moulded from years of emotional turmoil into seeing the world through a lens of negativity, doom and gloom, panic, and anxiety, so give yourself time to recover and to get back to a more positive and forward-looking state of mind. This takes time, but once you stop gambling, the recovery starts. You need to elicit all your energies and resources in focusing on the primary objective of stopping all gambling activities. I will guide you on how to deal with the consequences of opening up to your gambling addiction in phases two and three, but for the first ten days, it is imperative that you do not gamble. Inordinate willpower will be needed, especially in avoiding betting establishments, not logging on to betting websites or mobile betting applications, not buying scratch cards, not playing lotto or bingo, and so on.

Willpower does imply a sacrifice of something good. Gambling is not good, but from my own experience, the first few weeks do entail a lot of focus and willpower to abstain from betting. But once you are firmly on the road to recovery, it will be less willpower and more the change of mind-set towards gambling coupled with stronger emotional and mental resolve that will sustain your recovery. Do not view giving up gambling as a sacrifice, but see giving up gambling as an enhancement to your life. You may feel your mind is racing out of control, but try to be calm and understand that this is normal and is part of your recovery. Boredom or indeed panic will arise, but so be it—be bored, I would suggest that you revisit the techniques for phase one to ensure that you address, manage, or prevent these feelings. If you apply the same energy you did to gambling in not gambling, you will overcome this addiction.

Finally, in this phase or indeed other phases, you may feel extremely tired, not just from stress but also from the emotional strain of dealing with a lot of issues. It is important to get sufficient rest. Do not rush through the programme. And talk to a partner, friends, family, or GA members about your lethargy. They will offer you the support you need to keep going, but keep in mind that lethargy is also part of your recovery.

**PLEASE DO NOT READ ON TO
PHASE TWO UNTIL YOU HAVE FINISHED
PHASE ONE.**

CHAPTER 4
Phase Two: ACCEPTANCE

4.1 Introduction

Well done on getting through phase one. You have proven to yourself that you can stop gambling for a period of time. If you can do it for ten days, you can do it forever. Leaving everything else aside, this is a phenomenal achievement. As we recovering problem gamblers know, all too well, how difficult it is to liberate oneself from the straitjacket of gambling, this is a milestone in your life. When I reached ten days, I said, "Let's drive on now and maintain the momentum gained." It is important not to get complacent; gambling addiction is an insidious condition and will attempt to creep up and grab you when you are least aware, so be vigilant. Now let's work on the achievements of phase one in working through phase two.

Duration: Five days (day eleven to day fifteen)

On successful completion of phase two of the "SAFEstep™" method "Acceptance", it is important to reward yourself. This can be a meal out with your spouse or partner, treat yourself to a new item of clothes, meet a friend for a coffee, an overnight stay in the country, go bowling with friends, go to the movies, and so on. While finances may be very tight, allocate some budget and/or time for this reward. Agree this with a partner, spouse, family member, or friend.

4.2 Objectives of phase two

- Feel more at ease in acceptance of the consequences of your gambling and the events that may follow.
- Manage and deal more effectively with the feelings associated with the consequences of your gambling.
- Become better equipped, emotionally and mentally, to enter phase three.

It is important to note that the techniques and tools that you used in phase one to stop gambling; are as important in this phase as they were in phase one. So continue to practice those techniques that worked for you in phase one. Again, you may need to adopt more of the techniques or alternatively change what you are doing to ensure that you maintain momentum in this phase. So for example, if exercise is working for you, consider spending a bit more time running, cycling, or going to the gym; or if you find Gamblers Anonymous a huge help, then continue attending (more meetings if you feel you need to); or if you find that not having access to credit cards and cash is helping, then continue the arrangement with your confidante, friend, or family member.

As this phase's title suggests, you need to accept things as they are now. George Orwell once said, "Happiness can exist only in acceptance." Acceptance is the basis of all action, and unless you fully allow and accept your current situation then you cannot act and start changing things for the better. What we resist persists, so learn to fully accept your current situation. Do not resist, do not challenge, and do not judge what your situation is today as a result and consequence of your gambling behaviour. It is important to note that acceptance is not submission, but simply an acknowledgment that all your actions have consequences, and that you need to take responsibility for those actions and consequences. How you react to these consequences is your choice, but by reacting in a positive and responsible manner, this will lead to your recovery and future happiness. Acceptance also does not mean you have to accept the unacceptable; for example, if you are pressured into doing a criminal act to write off a debt or asked to agree to punitive interest rates on loans, then do not accept. Acceptance here means acknowledging a situation and taking honest and proper responsibility for it. Buddha said "It is your resistance to 'what is' that causes your suffering." If you resist and think you can solve your financial woes by going back to gambling, you are not accepting. If you plead with your partner to take you back now, you are not accepting. If you continue to fraudulently or deceitfully take money from an employer, spouse, or partner, then you are not accepting but trying to resist reality. This will only exacerbate an already difficult and volatile situation. However, accepting will allow you to shed a large emotional and mental burden, and it will allow you exit phase two and go on to phase three and sustain recovery.

It will be difficult to accept certain situations, situations that will be deemed by much of society as morally and ethically wrong and in many cases may have been criminal actions. You may feel shame, guilt, and embarrassment in owning up and accepting the consequences of your actions during your gambling addiction. It is imperative to remember that by owning up to and being responsible for your actions (for possibly the first time in a long time) you are taking a huge step forward on your road to recovery. Guilt, shame, embarrassment, anxiety, remorse, disgust, anger, and depression may be some of many emotions and feelings that will accompany you for some time, but this is normal. I will detail later how to address these potentially demotivating emotions and feelings that can stifle recovery.

Acceptance also brings awareness of your selfishness in ignoring the hurt you caused some people, and awareness of a life wasted looking at a ball spinning around a wheel, horses running around a racetrack, a ball popping out of a bingo chute, and greyhounds chasing a dummy hare. When you break it down, it is almost comical what adults get obsessed about. Not only that, but look what they spend all their money on as well—just think about it. Acceptance also brings awareness that you need to fix your problem, rebuild your life, and build bridges with loved ones.

Some examples, and by no means an exhaustive list, of consequences that may need to be accepted include:

- Criminal proceedings and possible imprisonment as result of serious fraud.
- Loss of your business.
- Loss of employment and career prospects, but a change of career may bring you more happiness.
- Loss of relationship with your spouse or partner.
- Alienation from your family and partner.
- Loss of social network (many friends may be gamblers).
- Loss of friends.
- Homelessness.
- Property (house, car, etc.) repossession.
- Health (mental, emotional, and physical) implications caused by years of intense stress.
- Financial distress and creditors chasing you for money.
- May receive lot of verbal abuse from partner, spouse, family, friends, or colleagues.
- Surrender of previous lifestyle (this may prove to be positive).

Reading these potential consequences may seem daunting, may frighten you, and may cause you great anxiety. The idea is not to cause you concern or anxiety but to allay your fears; most problem gamblers have inevitably faced at least one, if not most, of these issues, and they have recovered and rebuilt their lives. Gamblers have a propensity to magnify their problems, making these issues almost insurmountable and debilitating in the eyes of a gambler. Although the problems appear daunting, they can, have, and will be overcome and will pass in time. Most of these consequences may be temporary.

Once your life is taken back from the addiction of gambling, you can work on rebuilding relationships that were damaged, connecting with family and friends, going back to work, and paying back creditors. Again, remember, you will become a stronger, better, and more appreciative person during and after recovery. It all awaits you.

Phase three of the "SAFEstep™" method, "Functioning and Economy," will help you deal in a structured, straightforward, and programmatic way with many of the financial, emotional, relational, and familial issues caused by your out-of-control gambling.

4.3 Recommended coping techniques for phase two

The acceptance phase is critical for you to move on with your recovery. Again, facing up and taking responsibility for your actions as a result of your gambling will elicit a lot of emotional strain and mental anguish, but it is a stepping-stone to recovery. Here are some tips and techniques to assist you. Remember to continue with those coping techniques in phase one that work and are stopping you from gambling.

- Understand that the consequences of your gambling behaviours exist and need to be faced. Letting go of your attachment to social status and objects such as cars, houses, the latest phones, TVs, and so on will help you through this phase. Social status, approval of others or material objects will never define you or make you complete; only you can do that. Yongey Rinpoche states, in his book *The Joy of Living*, "When our mind is conditioned by attachment, we lose the ability to distinguish between the bare experience of happiness and whatever objects temporarily makes us happy." A huge burden will be lifted from your shoulders once you realise and accept that what unfolds will take its own course. While it may be unpleasant, it will be a massive step forward on your road to recovery and normal life. In his book *Man's Search for Meaning,* Viktor E. Frankl wrote, "Everything can be taken from a man but one thing: the last of the human freedoms—to choose one's attitude in any given set of circumstances, to choose one's own way." While you may lose material possessions, friends, and/or lose a relationship with a spouse or partner, you ultimately choose how you respond to these situations and events. Why wallow in self-pity when you can decide to respond and think positively? See this as an opportunity to do new things, meet new people, and experience a whole new, different and rewarding life.

- Do not follow the train of thought that comes when thinking of the potential consequences of your gambling; stop the thought in its tracks. It is a tendency of gamblers to dramatize and think of worst-case scenarios; this will only cause you more stress. *Acknowledge* the thought, *observe* the thought, and *dismiss* it. You cannot dictate the outcome of events; yes, you can manage them, but do not try to alter them, which is resistance and not acceptance. Remember, whatever happens will strengthen your resolve from an emotional and mental perspective, but only if you accept what has happened and are willing to accept the consequences.
- See each day as another stepping-stone to recovery. People will begin to admire your resolve in taking responsibility and dealing with issues. Those people who mind do not matter and those who matter do not mind. Keep strong and resilient, and just take it day by day.
- Learn to deal with the fact that life now may not be as exciting or as fast-paced as it was during your gambling years. However, once you start rebuilding your life and exploring new activities, interests and hobbies, you will develop a healthier, happier and brighter outlook on life; which will be worth more than any amount of excitement you got from gambling, and without the mental, emotional and financial pain.

- Impatience, impulsivity, and lack of tolerance are almost universal characteristics of all problem gamblers. These traits can cause you to rush through recovery and try to deal with consequences quickly. There is no shortcut to recovery, and dealing with these traits will require fortitude and understanding on your behalf. When you feel the urge to rush, don't. Rather, step back, take a deep breath, and be still until you better understand what you are doing and why you are doing it.
- Feelings of shame, ignominy, anger, disgust, embarrassment, and regret will well up in you on a daily, hourly, and almost minute-by-minute basis. This actually reflects a genuine, honest, and empathetic character whose actions, which belied your true character, caused you to err. Again, observe these feelings non-judgmentally, how they manifest in your body and the emotions they arouse. In this instance, be a spectator of these thoughts and emotions; do not resist them, but let them be and let them pass through you and dissolve away. It will take time to lessen the impact these feelings have on you, but their strength will weaken and dissipate over time and allow you to deal more adequately with events, situations, and urges, and give you the mental resolve to move on to phase three. A useful tip here is to see yourself watching a movie: your thoughts, feelings, emotions, and behaviours are images represented on the screen; you are just an observer and not an active participant. Just be calm, observe, and let the images pass from scene to scene. Change the movie from a horror movie to a comedy, most of what we worry about never comes to pass, and those things that we do have to deal with, we handle an awful lot better than we expected.
- It is normal to compare and contrast your life with that of those people around you. Resist the urge to do this. You may feel inadequate and inferior, and that you have failed in life. Trust me, overcoming a gambling addiction will be a

phenomenal achievement, and no matter what material wealth another person has, remember that these material things are only transitory objects and do not last forever, indeed nothing lasts forever so do not dwell on it. Your success will stand the test of time, and you will become a stronger, wiser, and more appreciative person as a result of overcoming your gambling addiction. As Eleanor Roosevelt said, "Only a man's character is the real criterion of worth." Your character, overcoming a serious addiction, is growing stronger by the day.
- At all times be yourself, the English philosopher, Alan Watts wrote, "When a man no longer confuses himself with the definition of himself that others have given him, he is at once universal and unique." So do not pigeon-hole yourself as a particular stereotype or label that others may use such as "former gambler", "failed business man", "likes a bet" and so on, that is their issue not yours.
- Being judgemental or critical can be a form of non-acceptance. Ask yourself "What, who and why I am judging or being critical of?" Usually it is your own unhappiness and frustration that causes you to judge others, situations, and events. Take a few deep breaths and be open, receptive, compassionate and accommodating to the person, event or thing you are judging. You will find your attitude and perspective will change. Be open-minded, that person or event could bring great joy, happiness, and value to your life.
- Be patient. Shakespeare wrote, "How poor are they that have not patience! What wound did ever heal but by degrees?" Patience is not a trait of most problem gamblers. It will take some time for you to see improvements in your life. Observe the small but positive changes as you work through your recovery—improved mood, less anxiety, improved finances, feeling more composed and so on. Practice patience when

PHASE TWO: ACCEPTANCE

- stuck in traffic, standing in a queue, waiting for a response from somebody and so on.
- Accept also that there are people, things and situations in life that you can never control or direct, and is a waste of time and effort trying to influence or change them. Gamblers Anonymous have adopted the "Serenity Prayer," authored by the American theologian Reinhold Niebuhr at their meetings and is relevant here.

    "God, grant me the serenity to accept the things I cannot change,
    The courage to change the things I can,
    And the wisdom to know the difference."
- Read through the chapters covering phase one and phase two of the recovery programme every day.

**PLEASE DO NOT READ ON TO
PHASE THREE UNTIL YOU HAVE FINISHED
PHASE TWO.**

CHAPTER 5
Phase Three: FUNCTIONING and ECONOMY

5.1 Introduction

Brilliant! A hearty well done on getting to phase three. You have reached the fifteen day mark. This is a watershed on your road to recovery. For now, take a step back and think of the last time you were fifteen days free of a bet. Feel the inner pride of reaching this mark and pat yourself on your back for having battled through possibly the toughest fifteen days of your life so far. OK, you might be under a lot of strain regarding finances, relationship issues, legal issues, and work issues, but this phase and the "Pillar" chapter will elaborate a bit more on how to deal with these issues in a structured and programmatic manner.

Remember, it is critical that you continue using the coping techniques you learned in phase one and phase two and carry them into phase three. Do not be complacent and feel you have this nailed; the gambling condition will fool you into thinking that and will lull you into a false sense of security. Be vigilant and make sure you stick rigidly to or indeed expand on the coping techniques learned.

The functioning aspect of this phase refers to the coping strategies to help you deal with negative moods and emotions, legal issues, problems, and irrational thinking. The economy aspect refers to coping strategies for dealing with financial issues.

On successful completion of this phase, many gamblers who have worked the programme, refer, as needed, to the various coping strategies used in this book. If for example on a specific day you are dealing with some problems that are causing you strain and stress, then referring and consulting the "Dealing with problems" section(5.6) of this book will help in the management and resolution of whatever issues may be bothering you. It as an ongoing process and healing takes time, but once you have access to the correct tools and techniques then the journey is made easier and relapse to gambling avoided.

Duration: Fifteen Days (day sixteen to day thirty)

As with previous phases, on successful completion of phase three of the "SAFEstep™" method "Functioning and Economy", it is important to reward yourself. This can be a meal out with your spouse or partner, treat yourself to a new item of clothes, meet a friend for a coffee, an overnight stay in the country, go bowling with friends, go to the movies, and so on. While finances may be very tight, allocate some budget and/or time for this reward. Agree this with a partner, spouse, family member, or friend.

The tools and techniques below will help you in sustaining and maintaining your recovery. Identify what areas are causing you most difficulty and read the appropriate coping technique for that problem. Do not pressure yourself to deal with all issues now. Just take it one day at a time. You will, as time goes by, slowly become more adept and confident in dealing with issues as they arise.

Up to now, you have stopped gambling for fifteen days. This is a momentous occasion, and you have arrested the decline, chaos, madness, and mayhem that was destroying all the good in your life. WELL DONE, YOU! You are using the coping techniques to stop gambling, you accept your situation, and are better able to control and manage your gambling urges. You will need to revisit on a daily basis where issues arise and what you did to deal with them. This will continue well after your thirty days, and as your life becomes less chaotic and more structured, you can start doing more activities and start dealing more competently with issues that arise.

PHASE THREE: FUNCTIONING AND ECONOMY

This section will look at those issues that arose from your uncontrollable gambling and have not yet been addressed, and it will provide advice on how to manage them. The first two phases addressed the management and coping strategies around the urge to bet. It would have been unwise to try to deal with financial, emotional, legal, and relational issues as well, as it would, in my view, have been too much to handle in the early days of recovery. The programme follows a prioritised set of goals, and once you have a handle on the urge to bet, then you can competently deal with other issues caused by your time gambling. *Important also to continue using the coping techniques used and perfected in the first two phases of the recovery programme.* Also, please reference the website **www.how-to-stop-gambling.com**, where you can find the worksheet templates used in this programme, video diaries, blogs, discussion forums, FAQ's etc.

We will look at coping techniques for financial and legal affairs, relationship issues, problem solving, emotional and mood issues. These coping techniques are guides only and will offer advice on what to do or whom to consult with. It is important not to feel overwhelmed, so take one issue at a time. If you are feeling stressed, then stop and just concentrate on developing the techniques learned in previous phases until you feel more equipped to deal with other issues. It is recommended that you take one area at a time; coping with financial issues may be more of a priority for some, but the important thing is to not overwhelm yourself. You will have a lot of time to deal with these issues. Be patient (not a trait of many gamblers) and tolerant of those who pressure you. It is recommended you spend three days on each coping strategy and perfect the approaches used in the various coping techniques.

A gambler's life is invariably chaotic, and your thought and behaviour patterns reflect that chaos. It will take time to learn to think in a more structured and calmer way and to be able to prioritise issues as they arise. Do not beat yourself up for getting things wrong. You do not need to be perfect. We all screw up, so just learn from and laugh at your mistakes as you adopt and develop these coping techniques.

Finally, before you read on, I want you to adopt a ruthlessness that you may not have adopted before. What do I mean by ruthlessness? I mean being more genuine and caring to your core needs and not being dictated to or bullied by anyone else or living other people's expectations. This does not mean being selfish, but if any action or deed makes you feel pressured or uncomfortable, then do not do it. It also means being ruthless with creditors, and by that I mean, being honest about what you can and cannot pay and being ruthless in meeting payments when you commit to them. You must be ruthless with yourself and others, put activities and events in your diary, agree with others (if it is a group event), stick to your plans, and think long-term in your planning. Gamblers' planning never goes beyond the next betting event, and putting certain events and activities in the diary will keep you and others honest. You should be ruthless when you are bored and feel you are missing out on life; that is, you tell yourself there are many things you can do for nothing, so be ruthless in finding out about them and doing them. Start living your life. Ruthlessness here does not mean pulling a fast one on other people, sacrificing other people's happiness for your own, or exploiting or pressuring someone. Rather, it means being frank, open, honest, and committed to yourself and what you do.

5.2 Goals of phase three

- Cope competently with moods and negative emotions.
- Cope competently with financial issues.
- Cope competently with legal issues.
- Deal competently with problems.
- Deal competently with irrational thinking.

5.3 Coping with moods and negative emotions

During your gambling, you will have experienced a roller coaster of emotions and moods, from highs and joys of winning, to lows and the anger and despair of losing, to the pain of relationship breakups, to guilt and shame about things you did to feed your gambling addiction. So do you think that after years of this extreme conflict and extremes in emotional states, they will go away once you stop gambling? Of course not. You have developed hardwired reactions in your brain to events—losing or winning—and unbeknown to yourself, they have become automatic. For example, you lose, and you become moody, distant, irritable, or erratic, and if you win, you are elated, overly spontaneous, and prone to overspending. From my experience during recovery, these reactions could even get worse for a period of time and also be accompanied by extreme lethargy and fatigue. However, you should see this as part of your recovery.

Gamblers by nature often exhibit the following traits and symptoms of gambling (see how many you can relate to?):

- Impulsivity.
- Magnification of events and situations.
- Seeing situations as catastrophes and worst-case scenarios.
- Anxiety.
- Irritability, frustration, and agitation.
- Poor concentration and impoverished decision making.
- Extreme lethargy
- Sleeplessness.
- Social withdrawal and isolation.
- Personalisation of problems; that is, all problems are your fault and you and you alone are to blame.
- Projection of inner pain—the transfer of your inner turmoil to someone else; for example, you deem your partner to be the one with mood and emotional issues, and the one causing the strain on the relationship.

You may have some or all of these traits and symptoms, but remember you are improving daily. See the worsening of these traits and symptoms as a sign of recovery. Do not fight them, but be aware of them and aim to manage them better.

Emotions are a manifestation of your thoughts in your body. Your emotional reaction is your thoughts' energy source. The more you concentrate on and give attention to a thought, the more it sticks. So the key is to divert your attention and detach from the thought and its associated emotions. This does not mean suppress the negative thoughts, but to acknowledge the thought, observe the associated thoughts and feelings it creates, and say to yourself, "Ah, years of gambling have caused me to magnify thoughts and give far too much weight to their significance. But I am no longer going to be shocked or consumed by this thought." Smile at it and visualise the thought floating away from your awareness like a leaf in a stream. Do not worry if the thought still sticks or frightens you by its content; that is OK and normal. Just keep following the technique, and you will see that eventually the thoughts become less frequent and have less and less impact.

As mentioned earlier, during recovery you will become more aware of underlying issues. You should see a doctor, psychologist, or psychiatrist if you feel very depressed, morbid, or suicidal or suffer from extremes in emotions (highs and lows).

5.3.1 Coping techniques for moods and negative emotions

The following coping techniques will help you deal with some of the emotions and feelings you will encounter.

- Follow three simple steps here. First, **acknowledge** that you are feeling anxious, irritable, angry, remorseful, embarrassed, guilty, down, or feeling self-pity, say "Hello" to that feeling or feelings. Second, **observe,** non-judgementally, the feeling, what thoughts you have with that feeling, and how the feeling manifests in your body for e.g., twitching, churning in stomach, restlessness, trembling, raised blood pressure, blushing, heart palpitating, fatigue, or tears and so on. Third, slowly let the feeling **subside** and thoughts **dissolve**; the more you question or concentrate on why you feel or think this way, the more the feeling or emotion will grow, giving more energy to the thought. Just let the thought be and dismiss it. Have you ever tried to submerge a ball under water? The more you press down on it, the quicker it pops to the surface. Thoughts are the same, so instead of trying to repel it, just let it be, and like a ball on the water, it will float away in its own good time. To help here, think of a positive emotion. For example, if you feel anxious or angry, go with it as described above, and as the feeling dissipates, tell yourself it is time to feel calm and then just be calm, you can use the breathing exercises described earlier.

- Negative emotions can be caused by irrational thinking like "My boss or partner spoke unfavourably about me to a mutual friend today, and I feel angry and depressed over it." Now change it around and say, "What another person does or says about me is none of my business, and I cannot change or control what they think," and dismiss the thoughts and feelings associated with it. Another thought could be, "My new girlfriend did not text me back in a day; she must be tired of me already, and it goes to show how useless I am in relationships." This is you turning the situation into a worst-case scenario. Instead, turn this around and say, "With most relationships, especially in early stages, there are huge time gaps between correspondences; this is normal, and she will text me in her own good time." Again, observe your magnification of issues and say, "Ah, well, that is the gambler in me," and smile because the gambler in you will be leaving sometime in the future. Gamblers can feel angry over people's reactions or behaviours towards them. In this instance, just remember that you can only control *your* behaviours and not anyone else's. So as long as you stay composed and calm, eventually people will change their attitudes and act differently towards you. As Mahatma Gandhi said, "You must be the change you wish to see in the world."

- None of us are perfect, and you are undergoing a life-changing process that most people do not have to go through, so be easy on yourself. Gamblers have an inherent trait of wanting to control everything, or they think that everything must be perfect (*all or nothing*). Putting so much pressure on yourself will make you feel frustrated, irritable, and stressed. Embrace everything you do with fun; if you do it wrong, so what? If you feel embarrassed, be embarrassed and observe the bodily sensations that accompany it, like blushing and sweating, and say to yourself, "Hey, I am alive. My body is reacting this way. Isn't the body amazing? I want more of this." Remember also that it is OK to say no; do not do something you feel unhappy about doing. Also, gamblers are impulsive, so do not act in haste or speak or act in a rash way. Every time you feel emotional, angry, or upset, STOP, do nothing, and walk away from the situation or person; smile and say, "There is the gambler in me, but he (or she) no longer controls me." By not reacting in an impulsive way, you are showing who is boss.
- Remember that everyone at some stage experiences negative feelings about themselves or others. However, we have the choice whether to indulge and get consumed by them or to acknowledge the feelings and detach from them.
- Every time you feel anxious or stressed, instead of coming up with "What If?" type scenarios replace the words "What If?" with "So What?" This can be a powerful aid. For example,

PHASE THREE: FUNCTIONING AND ECONOMY

"What if I lose my job due to fraud committed to fund my gambling?" replace with *"So what if I lose my job? Many employers understand that talented people, like me, can fall foul to addiction, and are willing to give people another chance. There are many employers out there who would readily hire a person, who has given up gambling, like me. I have a lot to offer and now that am free of addiction will demonstrate that to my next employer."* Or *"What if my friends disown me for being so deceitful and getting big loans off them under false pretences?"* replace with *"So what if I lose the friendship of some people? Those that matter do not mind and those that mind do not matter. Real friends will stick by you in your hour of need and think of all the more enduring friendships you will gain by participating in new activities."*

The vast majority, in fact nearly all, of things or events that happen in our lives never play out as it does in our mind. Our mind will exaggerate and magnify issues, which invariably lead to stress and anxiety. If you can unconditionally accept what happens is meant to happen and happens for a reason so that you can learn, develop and grow as a person, then life will be a lot more manageable and enjoyable. This applies to all issues such as legal summonses, relationship breakdown, financial issues, emotional issues, and so on. No matter how bad a situation seems, ask not "why me?" but replace with "what am I going to learn and how am I going to develop from this crisis or situation?"

- Embrace your fear. We can spend our lives living in fear, fearing that we will not get what we want or fearing that we will lose what we have gained. Fear is an illusion and the more you embrace it, the greater will be your strength. Use the energy of fear to your advantage to empower and liberate yourself.
- Resist the urge to always be right about something or someone. Holding your ground and defending your position can expend a lot of your energies, energies that could be used in more

productive activities and pursuits. Make your point and move on and just because you prove someone wrong does not make you right. Do not be a slave to your opinions and assumptions.
- When participating in something you like doing like swimming, jogging, renovating, gardening, reading and so on, you may still feel low, your mind racing, and your emotions contorted in a knot of pain. Continue what you are doing and again, just try and detach from getting caught up with the feelings. Change can be imperceptible but keep doing positive and good things and those negative feelings, emotions, and thoughts will go in time.
- When you are having a bad day, just say to yourself "During recovery I will have bad days, but a lot more good days. This is one bad day off the list, so lots more good days to come." During the bad days, try and concentrate on one positive aspect of your life such as improved physical health, developing new skills, improving finances and so on, this will help you change your negative mind-set to a positive one.
- Once you have your emotions under control, try and understand and explore the causes and reasons for your emotions by using the cause, effect and action technique below. Use the emotional analysis worksheet (Appendix 6) as a guide.

Example:

Cause:
Your spouse referred to fact that finances are in perilous situation and that the annual holiday abroad for the family is not going ahead this year.

Effect:
You might feel emotions of guilt at preventing your family from going on holiday, feelings of anger at yourself for allowing this

to happen, feelings of inadequacy for not being able to provide a holiday for your family or indeed anxiety in that your family may think less of you.

Action:
Use the **SIR** approach here.
Step back from emotions.
Identify the root cause for the emotion and
Rationalise it.

So in the case above.

Step back from the feelings of guilt, anger, and anxiety. Use the deep breathing techniques learnt previously. Do not act on the feelings or emotions. *Identify* the root cause. In this case: your spouse indirectly causing you some emotional pain by referring to a sensitive topic. *Rationalise it*. Yes, you have put the family finances in bad shape as a result of your gambling. However, you are slowly working to repair the damage done. Trust me, your spouse and family will be very proud of you; if not today, sometime in the future when they realise the battle you have fought and won. Yes, holidays are nice and something to look forward to. However, it is not where you go but how you spend time with your family that counts. There may be an alternative cheaper low cost option to go somewhere in your own country for a few days or if not, then spend time doing things at home with your family like going for a meal out one evening, going to a play, cinema or theatre together, having a small party at home. It is being there for your family and listening to their own issues and pains, and showing and giving them your love and attention that matters most, not going on holidays abroad. Is it really that terrible you cannot go on a holiday? Absolutely not, but by feeling guilty, anxious or angry it will only divert your energies away from your own recovery. Be compassionate to people who may have aroused negative emotions in you, that will help you to manage your emotions better and demonstrate to the other person you are on the road to recovery. Remember, you are on the path of recovery and that is all that matters right now. Be compassionate and kind to yourself also and praise yourself, you are doing your level best and that is all one can ask.

- Meditation or deep breathing can only help in recovery. We covered an aspect of deep breathing in phase one (dealing with general gambling urges technique). There are plenty of books, guides, and centres that guide and practice meditation, mindfulness, yoga, Pilates, and so on that you can read up on. If any of these work for you, then get more involved. I have outlined a simple meditation exercise that I do for fifteen minutes twice a day. Recovering problem gamblers' minds are in a constant state of churn and flux, so it may take a while before you can sit still for fifteen minutes. Start with one minute and work your way up to longer sessions.
    - Sit still, back straight (without feeling uncomfortable), palms cupped or joined in each other, legs relaxed, and both soles touching floor. Adopt a position that is comfortable but not slouched.
    - Do nothing for a minute.
    - Slowly observe your breath entering your nostrils; imagine it circulating like a stream going around your skull, down around your spine, into your lungs, and deep into your abdomen. As you breathe in, expand your tummy and fill your abdomen with air. Do not do this forcefully or take big gulps of air; just breathe nice and relaxed. Let everything—your mental anguish, your difficulties, your anxiety—be exactly as it is and not be distracted by it during this exercise.

- Exhale every ounce of breath through your mouth; imagine it tapering off into the distance. Deflate your tummy when breathing out. Feel your body relaxing and your mind slowing down.
- Do this for as long as possible, one to fifteen minutes, however long you can. Your mind will wander; let it wander, but slowly bring your focus back on your breath and repeat. Also, observe bodily sensations as you breathe in and out.
- You will feel frustrated as the mind keeps wandering, but that is what the mind does. Do not resist, and when you can, bring focus slowly back to inhaling and exhaling.
- If your mind wanders, then observe it wandering. That is also being mindful.
- That is it!

- In his book *The Road Less Travelled*, M. Scott Peck refers to a concept of bracketing whereby you put aside all prejudices, judgments, and biases when dealing with an event, person, or situation. Gambling losses and the perceived missed opportunities in life may have soured your perceptions and judgments of people, events, or situations. See your recovery as a new beginning. The people or things you deemed were of no value to you before might all of a sudden open up a whole new vista of opportunities and possibilities. Simply be open and embrace change. Try new things, but most importantly do not judge any person, action, event, or situation.
- Many emotional problems are caused by being over concerned about ourselves. We believe our worries are like no others, that you need to give all your time and attention to yourself and you can spend hours upon hours ruminating and worrying about yourself. I will be frank, your worries and concerns pale into insignificance in the greater scheme

of things. There are many people better off than you, yes for sure, but there are a lot more worse off; who have to deal with unimaginable crisis, pain, grief and who live in intolerable conditions. So a useful piece of advice is to worry about and have concern for other people, and how you can in some way alleviate the suffering they are enduring. Some examples of this are to help a recovering gambler, undertake volunteer work at a local community group, do a charity run or cycle for a good cause and so on.

- Strong feelings of anger may still reside within some recovering problem gamblers. Most of this may be self-directed and in some cases directed towards others. This anger may be related to feeling stuck, frustrated, guilty, ignored, or criticised. *However, it is highly important not to act on these feelings.* It will help to follow the same steps as detailed above in acknowledging and observing the feelings of anger and letting the feelings subside. Accept that anger is, understandably, going to accompany you on your journey through recovery for some time, but once you dissociate with, let go of, and break your connection with the angry feelings, they will dissipate and no longer control you. Be compassionate to your anger, smile at it, concentrate on your breathing (use meditation techniques above) and recognise that soon it will pass. Do not follow the thoughts that go with the angry feelings, and if necessary leave the place, event, or person that may be causing these feelings in you. Shame and feelings of inadequacy may be a factor in your anger. These are thoughts linked to erroneous beliefs and assumptions, but they are not true. Everyone at some point in their life feels insecure, inadequate, ashamed, guilty, and frustrated, but the key is to embrace these normal human feelings and not react to them. The Buddhist master Thich Nhat Hanh wrote, "If you allow compassion to spring from your heart, the fire of anger will die straight away." Focus

the energy generated by your anger into doing something good and beneficial for you and others—make good out of bad.
- Feelings of guilt may also linger for a long time. Guilt for the harm caused to loved ones due to your behaviours and actions during your gambling addiction. Guilt at the emotional scars and financial damage you may have caused to your family, partner, or friends. Guilt at being selfish and irresponsible. However, let me state clearly, guilt requires some emotional capacity for caring and compassion. If you do not possess empathy and sympathy for others, it will be difficult to feel guilt. Guilt indicates that you have a well of love, empathy, sympathy, care, and compassion for others. Take your thoughts of guilt and transform them into feelings of love and compassion for others; soon feelings of guilt will subside as others see the real, caring, and compassionate you.
- Finally, talk with someone you can open up to about your feelings; it can be a friend, a partner, a GA member, or a psychologist. Do not hold these feelings in; let them out and people will listen. It is OK NOT TO BE OK.

5.4 Coping with financial pressures

It is almost inevitable that the majority of gamblers will have a heavy financial debt burden after their gambling exploits. This probably is the biggest single factor in gamblers relapsing into a life of gambling and further pain and misery. It is imperative that you adopt a coping technique around your finances, so that you do not relapse and return to the clutches of this debilitating condition.

The amount of debt is relative; you might owe a few thousand or a few million, but the pressure felt can be the same for each individual with gambling debt. Owing money can bleed you of every ounce of self-respect and self-esteem, but you should realise that most people owe money. You probably asked people you regret asking or did things you regret doing, but accept that. Once you start dealing with your debt, even in small steps, your self-respect and self-esteem will return stronger than ever. It is important to note here that once you stop gambling, the haemorrhaging of money will stop. Although there will be a lot of healing and repayments to be made, you have started the process. The techniques below will assist you in that process.

Be resilient and steadfast here in dealing with creditors; you owe them, so they need to worry about you. Approach all debt with a business-like attitude and remove all emotion. You need to feed yourself, clothe yourself, and keep a roof over your head; these are essential items you need to pay for before anybody else gets a cent. Yes, there will be pain, legal notices, verbal abuse, and possibly threats, but it is a simple approach. You can only pay what you have after your core living expenses are met, and all creditors will have to live with that fact. It is also very important to assume responsibility for your debt yourself. Up to now, you may have brushed your responsibility under the carpet. It is not that complicated, and most people will discuss calmly and prudently with you about how the debt can be paid, but you need to take the initiative. The following techniques will help.

5.4.1 Coping techniques for managing debt

- Up to now, dealing with debt was in the now. You felt as if you had to pay everyone now, and you had to move quickly and get money as quickly as possible. Your horizon did not extend beyond the next race, the next spin of the wheel or slots, the next hand of cards. But you need to view debt repayment over months, years, or decades. If you spread your debt over, say, five, ten, or fifteen years, then all of a sudden the burden becomes manageable. The key is to pay off small portions that

are within your repayment capacity. Keep that in mind during all negotiations with creditors, both personal and institutional.
- Use the urge-suppression techniques outlined in phase one, "Stability," if the urge to gamble, because of financial problems, is great.
- View debt over years not weeks or months. It may take you decades to pay back debt, so be it, but by spreading the debt over years, indeed decades, it will make it far more manageable and less of a burden.
- Accept that you will have to sacrifice many things. You may well have to make lifestyle changes like no more holidays, no more perks, and start living within your means, to name but a few. You may be hassled, possibly accompanied with verbal abuse, by those you owe money to, but remember, this will bring a lot of positives—you will know who your true friends are, and you will become more confident in dealing with financial pressures and issues. You will explore a new lifestyle that will be better and more fun for you, and you will become more tolerant and resilient as a result. Refer to phase two, "Acceptance," if you are struggling here with this coping technique.
- Debt owed to close friends and family is the most emotionally overbearing. My advice here is to talk to each person individually and work out a plan for repayment. This will not be easy, but my experience taught me that being brutally honest with people about how much, when, and how often you can repay is usually well received and appreciated by most people. Try to leave the emotion out of discussions, as it will not help you or the creditor. Also, you do not have to open up to everyone about your predicament. You may feel like offloading emotionally to people, but this may not always be the best option; keep it business-like. If after discussing a repayment plan, you are being threatened or continually harassed, then stick to what you can afford; in the majority of cases, the

bark of creditors is worse than their bite. Something is better than nothing, and remember that you owe them, so they have a vested interest in keeping you on their side. Report to the police or get legal advice in the case of threats of violence to you or your family, or threats of damage to personal or business property.

- Debt owed to financial institutions will inevitably be a burden on many recovering problem gamblers. During the times of easy credit where banks recklessly loaned money, debt accumulated via re-mortgaging, rescheduling of loans, pre-approved loans, 100 per cent mortgages, and so on. Banks are now pursuing people aggressively for monies owed, and lending has dried up (it's a shame banks were not as prudent in the days of easy credit). First, always make sure your core needs like food and bills are covered before agreeing with banks on repayment plans. Remember, while you gambled, a lot of the easy credit came your way. Banks were culpable too, and any repayment plan should be thoroughly negotiated. There are many options here, such as debt write-off, lower interest payments, payment breaks, extending terms of loan, parking of debt, and split mortgages to name but a few. If all avenues are exhausted, then refer to phase two and accept the outcome. Please reference the list of agencies that can help in dealing with banks and other financial institutions in Appendix 7.
- Make a full list or inventory of all your debt. Write it all down, from the largest to the smallest amount. Do not leave anything out. This may look daunting at first, but do not omit or hide any debt. To help here, refer to the financial summary worksheet in appendix 2; you can use this to list creditors (personal and institutional). This is broken down into five areas: total debt, total income, basic living expenses, amount you can repay, and a debt repayment schedule for creditors. This example is for a

month, but you can break it down weekly or even daily; it's up to you. Here are the steps:
- Fill out total debt; leave absolutely nothing out. It will actually be a relief to understand what you owe and to have something to work towards, irrespective of amount.
  - ➢ Assign a priority to each level of debt; e.g., personal loans **priority one** (must be paid as soon as possible; these might be loans from friends who need the money or high-interest personal loans); **priority two** (not urgent and may be able to renegotiate; e.g., mortgage, credit union loans); and **priority three** (can leave for longer term until financial situation stabilises; e.g., friends who are not in immediate need of money).
- Total up all income for the month.
- Make a full list of monthly bills, bank repayments, rent, mortgage, etc. that must be paid.
- Deduct total outgoings from income.
- Based on priority, divvy up excess money (if any) and pay creditors according to priority rating. It is important to review the financial summary each month and stick rigidly to it.
- This is the difficult part: review all items again and determine what has to go. Maybe the car? Get public transport. Maybe it is the cigarettes, Saturday nights out, or takeout food. Maybe you need to move to cheaper accommodation, go to prepay only on your mobile phone, get rid of premium TV services, and so on. You need to review all of what is called non-**essen**tial expenditures. This will be temporary until you get back to some financial stability. I suggest you review this weekly at a minimum and possibly daily if need be. You need to take some pain here and see it as a part of your recovery.

- Depending on your income and circumstances you may be eligible for mortgage interest supplement, mortgage interest tax relief, other occupation related tax relief and more. So ensure to check all your entitlements.
- It may be that you have no excess income to distribute to creditors for a few months. That is fine. Make sure you cover core expenses, and inform creditors that once your income situation improves, you will commence repayments. Be steadfast here and do not be bullied into paying back. Again, if there are any overt threats of violence to yourself, family, or property, report them to the police.
- Prioritise payments. The most important thing is to talk to each creditor, be it an institution or individual, and explain that your finances are rock bottom and that you need to negotiate your repayment schedule. There is no need to tell anyone outside of those closest to you why you are in this predicament. Retain all correspondence (e-mails, letters, legal notices, and so on) with financial institutions. Be honest with creditors, but under no circumstances prioritise creditors over your core needs such as rent, food, and essential bills. Once you have a clear picture of who gets what each month, stick rigidly to the repayment plan. Once you have stabilised the financial ship, you will gain a lot of pride in paying back people. Just get the process sorted out and started, and once in place, matters will get easier as weeks and months pass by.
- For larger loans such as secured debt, it will be advisable to talk with an attorney, financial consultant or debt agency to get guidance on how best to deal with that loan.
- It might be worth liaising with debt agencies that offer free advice like money advice and budgeting services, insolvency services, and so on. Contact details of some of these organisations are contained in Appendix 7.

PHASE THREE: FUNCTIONING AND ECONOMY

- Consider taking up a part-time job if appropriate to subvent your current income.
- Work through the financial summary worksheet and review at least every month.

All of this may be difficult initially, but it will eventually get easier. Be aware that if you smoke or drink heavily, it would be preferable to stop now. However, to do so may be too much too soon, so it's best to reduce your intake within reason and gradually reduce, if not eliminate, money spent on these items. Also, do not turn to loan sharks and expensive money lenders. Do get rid of all credit cards. If you need a credit card for some online purchases, then use prepaid credit cards only.

5.5 Coping with legal issues

Much like financial issues, legal issues need to be addressed in a business-like manner. Gambling's fuel is money; without it, gamblers cannot feed their addiction. When all legitimate sources of borrowings are exhausted, a gambler may turn to fraud or other illegal means to secure funds to feed his or her addiction. The scale of illegality can vary from stealing petty cash to large-scale corporate fraud and embezzlement. The spiral into crime, in most cases, is gradual; the deeper one gets into the mire, the worse the level of fraud becomes. You follow a path of complete and utter self-destruction. When the dust settles, you feel distraught and disbelieving at how you let this happen, and how an honest, genuine, and caring person could do such things. You cringe at the shame and ignominy you have brought on yourself and your family. STOP THERE.

Yes, what you did was wrong and may be criminal, but it is done. Accept that. Now there may well be consequences e.g., court proceedings, but at some point in the future this will be forgotten and you may well have made reparations to the injured parties. So for now, deal with legal issues in an unemotional and business-like way. By following the programme, you will one day make amends for your gambling addiction driven criminal behaviour. Those who matter will look beyond your illegal and desperate actions and know it was gambling that drove you to do what you did.

5.5.1 Coping strategies in dealing with legal issues

- Stop all illegal activity immediately. Do not think you can cover your tracks or eventually resolve the situation by continuing your illegal activity.
- Do not keep the heavy burden of your actions to yourself. Discuss with a confidante, partner, or GA member whom you can comfortably, openly, and honestly talk with.
- Take full responsibility for your actions. The sense of relief from an emotional and stress perspective will be enormous once you fully accept what you have done and whatever consequences that follow. Yes, you may have feelings of shame, ignominy, disbelief, anger, and guilt as a result of your actions. However, deal with these feelings using the relaxation and calming techniques used in phase one, "Stability". Remember also, in a few months all this will be all forgotten about. There are countless people who have rebuilt their lives and become very successful after dealing with the consequences of actions comparable, if not far worse, than yours.
- It is advised that you immediately seek legal advice if the crime is on a large scale. You should refer to an attorney if the budget allows. There are also many no-cost legal bodies that will assist you here. Please see Appendix 7 for more information. If paying for legal services, ensure you are clear on the

type of billing adopted by the attorney, for example, flat rate billing, per hour billing and so on.
- Do not panic and again act in a cool, calm and collected manner. Be honest and open with your legal advisor on the illegal act(s) committed, and let he or she guide you on next steps. Try and educate yourself on legal terminology, similar cases and so on, this will ensure you have a better understanding about what is going on.
- In some cases, it might be an option to come clean with the injured party (employer, colleague, partner, etc.) and commit to repay the funds embezzled. This may not always be the most recommended course of action. Please consult with a legal professional or agency for guidance here. See a list of agencies in Appendix 7. It will be a relief when you do eventually come clean, but it will be up to your discretion how and when you do this.

5.6 Dealing with problems

From my own experience, I found I tended to pile all my problems into one heap and think to myself, "This is impossible and too much to bear." This is especially true with finances. Gamblers tend to add up all debts (*magnify*), think they need to pay them now (*impulsive*), and inevitably bet heavily to try to win the money to pay back the debts. A more prudent approach would be to break down all problems and deal with smaller issues one at a time, as opposed to tackling one large issue. Over the years of gambling, gamblers tend to ignore a problem until it reaches a breaking point. Then they scurry to solve it, usually in a frantic manner that invariably causes more pain and suffering. I personally found the financial pressure intense at times, and getting access to money, salary, loans, and so on, had to be managed prudently and carefully. However, my attitude was always,

"I owe this money and I am determined to pay it back." This not only reduces amounts owed and takes heat off you, but it ensures that the gambling trigger of access to cash is dealt with quickly and will not trigger a relapse.

These skills will take time to develop, but practice makes perfect. You will slowly begin to tackle issues more prudently and pragmatically.

5.6.1 Coping techniques in dealing with problems

- Most problems can be solved. It is the magnification and impulsive reactions of gamblers that exacerbate and worsen problems, not help resolve them. View problems as a way of improving your coping skills and controlling your magnification and impulsive tendencies. Once you accept that there is a problem and you do all that you can to resolve it using the techniques below, you can rest easy knowing there was nothing more you could have done; you should not beat yourself up over the outcome if it did not go as expected. Problems should be embraced and as Hugh Miller once said, "Problems are only opportunities with thorns on them." Use problems as a means to learn new skills and develop better qualities. For example, if banks or creditors are chasing you for money, then by dealing with them you become more assertive and learn to negotiate better repayment plans. Another strategy might be learning new do-it-yourself skills so you can save money on house maintenance and repairs.
- Remember problems are always expected but never permanent. As Marcus Aurelius, the emperor of the Roman Empire said, "The impediment to action advances action. What stands in the way becomes the way." So instead of asking yourself "Why me?", ask "What is the universe teaching me here at

PHASE THREE: FUNCTIONING AND ECONOMY

this difficult time?". Flip it around and use the problem to your advantage.
- Break down all problems into categories such as financial issues, relationship issues, work issues, health issues, legal issues, and personal issues. Appendix 4 has a problem-solving worksheet you can use.
  - Now take one of these categories and break it down further. Let's use relationship issues as an example.
    - First **identify** one issue: arguing with your partner all the time.
    - **Define** this problem: arguing over finances, with your partner referring constantly to your gambling history.
    - **Propose a solution:** agree to have an "argue-free" time for the next few weeks or visit a relationship counsellor.
    - **Review** each option carefully and decide the best course of action: an "argue-free" time is better for now, as seeing a counsellor may be beyond your budgetary capacity.
    - **Evaluate** success of solution: Has it helped? If not, then ask yourself why and whether continuing the relationship is viable.
  - Take another issue such as a financial issue. You owe €3,000 to the bank.
    - **Identify** problem: you owe €3,000.
    - **Define** the problem: you owe €3,000 to your local bank.
    - **Propose a solution:** ask a friend for a loan or renegotiate with the bank to repay over a longer period.
    - **Review** each option: your friend has already done too much for you; this feels like old behaviour, and

> you still owe him €2,000, so going to the bank and renegotiating is the best option.
> ➤ **Evaluate** solution: the bank agreed, but this will mean you need to cut back further on some expenditure, such as getting rid of your TV package (you can do without having to watch football midweek). If the bank did not agree, then accept their position and let whatever process they initiate take its course.

- Once you decide on the approach to take in resolving or dealing with a problem, put that issue or problem aside. Park it and stop ruminating, worrying and fretting on it. Otherwise, it will consume your attention and energies.
- Common problems that recovering problem gamblers face include, unemployment, poor health, divorce, relationship break-up, worrying incessantly about health, finances, and so on. Apply the same technique, as above, in dealing with problems and put an action plan in place to resolve. For example, if unemployed, then see it as an opportunity to upskill, broaden skill base, retrain or go to college and start applying for jobs, or if in a lot of debt then use the "Coping with financial pressures" (Section 5.4) as a guide, or if going through a divorce or relationship breakup then talk through with family, friends or a professional counsellor.
- Do not be rushed in to making a decision, no matter what the problem is. Sometimes the best course may be to do nothing. Most people suffer from the *action bias*, that is, any action is better than no action at all, and that is not always the correct option. Evaluate all options in dealing with a problem. There are usually more options than just one or two, take your time and evaluate all options and once the decision is made, give all your energies in carrying out that decision; or if no decision is made let matters unfold and accept the outcome.

PHASE THREE: FUNCTIONING AND ECONOMY

- Do and concentrate on one problem and/or task at a time. Try and focus on one or two main priorities each day, by trying to achieve too much, you invariably achieve nothing.
- Using words like "wishing" and "hoping" in dealing with problems is a weak and negative approach. Use words like "want", "will", "would like", and commit and dedicate fully to whatever solution you decide upon.
- Eckhart Tolle in his book, *The Power of Now,* writes that people have only three options when presented with a troublesome situation or problem: they can change the situation, walk away from it or accept it. So keep this in mind when dealing with all problematic situations.
- Do not let perceived failures or self-doubts stop you from continuing to try and deal with problems. We usually get things wrong a lot more often than getting them right. So keep trying.
- Facing and dealing with people over sensitive issues like loans and monies owed can be energy sapping. Putting off dealing with these issues does not solve the problem. The best approach is to "bite the bullet," meet or call the person or institution in question, inform him or her of your current financial circumstance and agree a fair and doable resolution. Also, the problem, once tackled, is never as bad or difficult as it seemed, prior to discussing it.
- Some issues like legal or mental health issues may require professional treatment or advice. You can only do so much yourself. Depending on your financial situation, paying professionals may be beyond ability right now. However, there are plenty of organisations, help groups, support groups, and budgeting services that do not charge for their services. Some of these services are contained in Appendix 7. Please consult the list, and be aware that help is there for you.

5.7 Dealing with irrational thinking

Many negative thoughts and false beliefs are caused by irrational or distorted thinking. Gambling addicts are particularly prone to these thinking errors. These thinking errors can be summarised as follows:

- Mind reading: Believing you know how people think or feel about you e.g., "I can tell my partner hates me because of my gambling history."
- Magnification: Focus on one thing, event or situation and blow it out of all proportion and ignore the positive aspects e.g., "I completely messed up that interview, now will not get that or any other job, ever."
- Catastrophising: You expect worst case in everything and exaggerate the potential consequences, even though likelihood they will never happen for e.g., "This legal letter from the bank will lead to my ruin and I will lose everything."
- Generalising: You generalise the specific by deriving at a conclusion based on one specific event or situation. This is usually accompanied by the use of words such as "always", "everything", "anything", and "everyone" for e.g., you made a mistake doing that a task and you think "I cannot do anything right."
- All or nothing thinking: You think of everything in extremes for e.g., "Unless I get this job, I will never work again."
- Personalisation: You deem anything said or done refers in some way to you. For example, your partner mentions that finances are tight this month. You interpret this as a direct criticism and attack on you. Another form of personalisation is blaming yourself for other people's problems, for example, "My daughter's poor results at school are my entire fault due to my lack of attention to her schooling when I was gambling."
- Blaming: You perceive that other people or organisations are responsible for your issues and problems. For example, "My partner's attitude and behaviour to me caused me to gamble."

5.7.1 Coping strategies in dealing with irrational thinking

Your gambling may have caused a lot of duress and hardship to your family, friends, and colleagues, and you will feel obliged to go the extra mile to win back their trust. However, there is no need to feel you are at fault for normal life events that are totally independent of what you have done in the past. To adequately deal with negative thoughts and associated feelings and behaviours, it is worth considering the following points:

- What is the evidence that a certain thought is true? Verify it, and do not just make a broad statement that it is true because you think so. An example here is, "I am in so much debt that going back to gambling is the only option open to me to help make money." Ask for the evidence? It is clear that by gambling you got into this financial difficulty and to continue will make the situation even worse; by not gambling, you can reduce and eventually eliminate debt in time.
- Thoughts and facts may be completely different, so get the facts straight before you jump to any conclusions. For example, you get a missed call from a person you owe money to, so you automatically assume he is coming after you for the debt. Instead of assuming this, find out if it is true. Call him. It may be that he would like to know your current situation and how you both can work together in clearing the debt. If so, adopt the techniques outlined in section 5.4.1 on how to manage debt.
- Get the clear facts before making any judgement about a person or event. Put yourself in the other person's shoes and assume their position. Now think, how would you expect him or her to react? For example, you owe a friend a lot of money and you think he is being unfair for asking for an agreed repayment plan. By putting yourself in his or her position, you realise that it is totally fair and pragmatic; as he worked hard for that money and only fair he is paid back. Not only that, he

is accommodating you by spreading repayments out over a long period of time.
- Ask yourself, "Are there alternative explanations, and why do I assume there is only one possibility or course of action?" An example here would be that your partner wants to take a break from the relationship. You perceive this as an indication he or she wants to leave you for good and there is no going back. However, a break may give you both time to take a breather from the emotional roller-coaster and demonstrate how much you mean to each other. This may well strengthen the bonds of your relationship even further. The opposite of what you thought.
- Ask yourself. "What is the worst thing that can happen?" "Could I deal and live with it?" "Would this really matter in five years' time?" Asking yourself these questions will lessen the emotional reaction you might initially have.
- In some cases it might be worth asking yourself some of the following questions:
    - "Am I really certain about the situation or do I need to investigate further?"
    - "Am I jumping to conclusions here and being impulsive and rash in my reaction and judgement?"
    - "Is this really rational and normal thinking?" Be honest with yourself here.
    - "Do people really care if I make a mistake, look silly or act bit strange?" Not at all, most people not even notice.
    - "Doesn't everybody have a right to their own opinion and beliefs? Why should I try and convert them to my way of thinking?"
    - "Will this event or situation really have any material impact on my life?" Be practical and not over dramatic here.
    - "Are there other ways to look at this situation?"

PART II

CHAPTER 6
Pillars

6.1 Introduction

Once you are at thirty days and beyond, life, while it may still be difficult, will have settled somewhat for you. As you practice and develop your coping techniques, you will become more adept at dealing with life's issues and the impulses and urges that will invariably plague you for some time. These gambling impulses and urges will probably accompany you for the rest of your life, but they will gradually diminish over time if not go completely away. The "+ 1" of the "30+1 Day Recovery Programme" refers to each day of the rest of your life following on after the thirty-day recovery programme. Each day is one day further away from your last bet.

However, to complement your recovery, it is important that you build up what I call the pillars of your life. Let me explain.

If you wanted to support a structure, you would erect pillars, and they would be the support for the roof, ceiling, and so on. Imagine your life being the structure supported. You need to build up the pillars to ensure you have a stable structure that can weather any storm or event that comes across your path. The pillars in this case can be categorised into:

- Emotional pillar: peace of mind and emotional stability.
- Physical pillar: good health, healthy weight, fitness, etc.
- Spiritual pillar: what one does to nourish one's own spiritual well-being; whatever creed, race, or religion a person is.

- Personal development pillar: interests and hobbies.
- Work pillar: daily full-time, part-time, or volunteer work.
- Social network pillar: your social network of friends, family, and colleagues.
- Financial pillar: your current financial state, income and expenditure, savings, loans, debts to third parties and so on.
- Relationship pillar: this can refer to relationships with a partner, wife, husband, family, or friends.

However, we can also build up pillars that are not reliable, that will decay quickly and crumble—such as gambling—or we can spend all our energies and efforts on one pillar, such as committing to a relationship, to the detriment of developing other pillars, like developing new hobbies or meeting friends.

During the years of gambling, you probably have paid little heed to many of the important pillars. Rather, you worked on the bad pillars, like gambling, where most of your efforts would have gone. Now, let's take a look at this visually. Have a look at the two scenarios below. The first is a person who spends equal time, energy, and focus on the strong pillars of mental health, physical health, personal development, social network, spiritual, financial management, and relationships (scenario 1). The second person spends most of his time gambling and rest of time with his girlfriend, and does not work on other pillars (scenario 2). Assume for both people that there is a relationship breakup or loss of a partner, with the subsequent removal of the relationship pillar. What happens? In scenario one, there is a shakeup, but the structures stay in place. Even though there is pain at losing a partner, the other pillars will support the person through the tough time. But in scenario two, the person's whole life implodes and collapses, left in ruins and rubble, as the only supporting pillar is the weak pillar of gambling, which invariably collapses.

6.1.1 Scenario one

This person builds up his up solid emotional, physical, personal development, social, spiritual, financial, and relationships pillars.
LIFE YOU LEAD

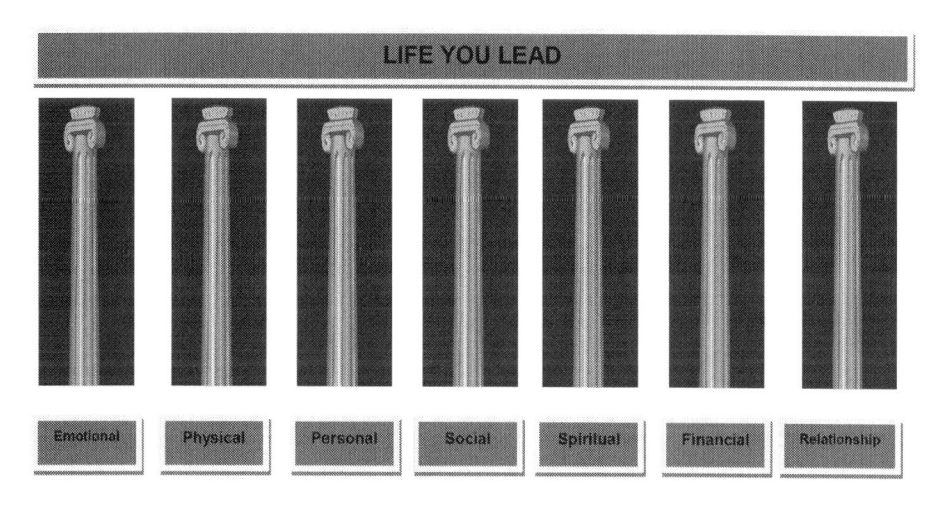

Now take away the relationship pillar. Although the structure is one pillar less, the stability in the person's life is assured with the solidity and support of the other pillars.

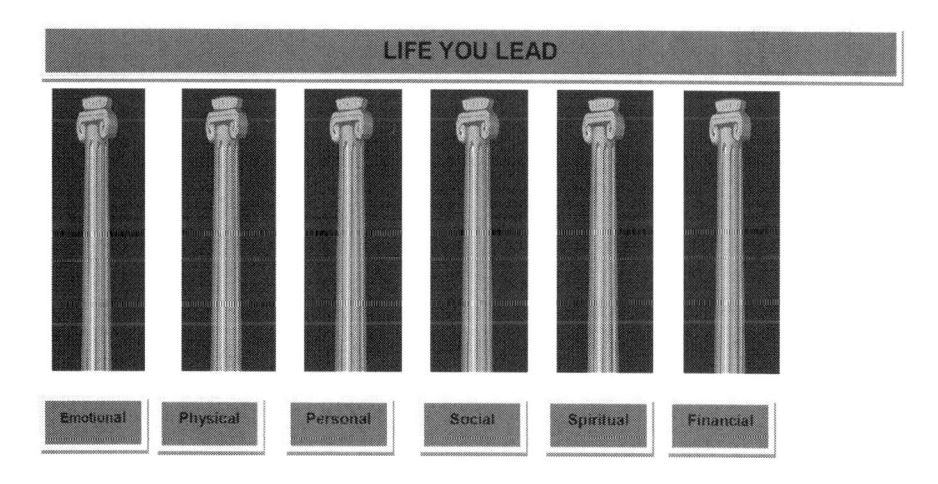

6.1.2 Scenario two

This person spends most of his time gambling and rest being with his girlfriend.

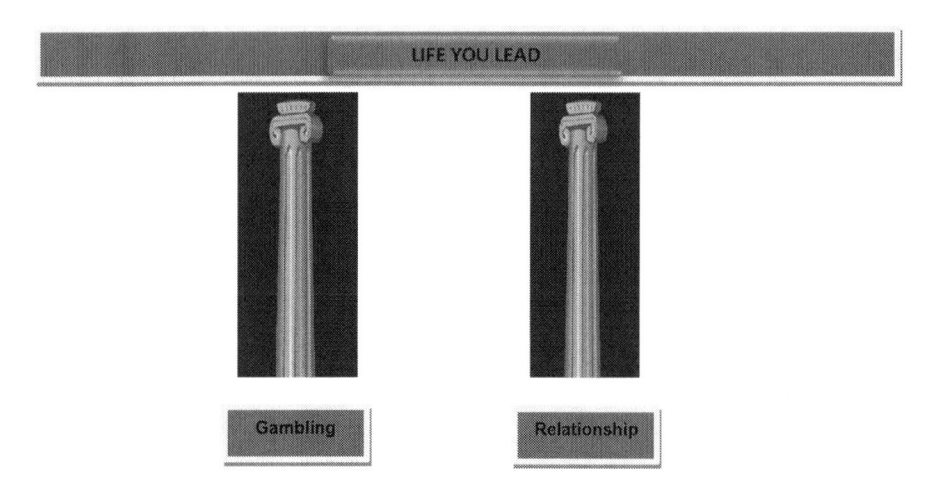

Now take away the relationship pillar and the life he leads collapses.

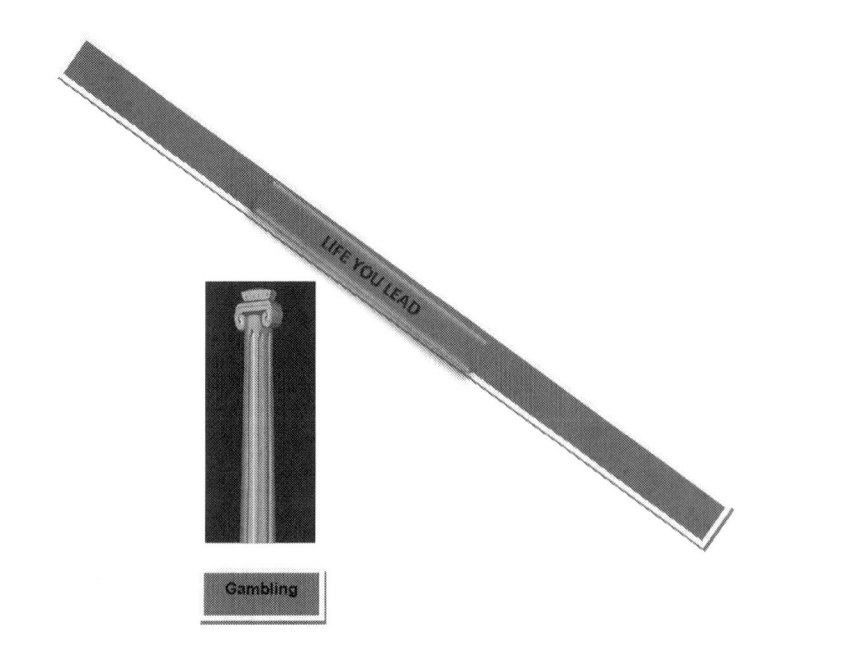

6.2 Pillar development

So, how do you ensure that you fortify and build up your pillars? Let's take each one in turn and look at the options. The important thing here is not to spend all your time on one pillar but move on to the next. It is about balance and spending time evenly across all pillars. I will go through each pillar in turn and give you ideas on how to develop them. Remember, there are many more options, so you can come up with your own. It is important also to remember to build them up slowly—do a small task like walking a mile, reading five pages of a book, or meditating for a few minutes. You do not need to run ten miles the first day or read a whole book in one day; just slowly ease into activities and approaches. You will have so much time now to develop these pillars—time that was previously spent wantonly on gambling.

As you engage in new activities, you may find some activities really of interest to you and would like to develop them further; you may want to start writing a book, join a cycling team, lead charity fundraising events, learn a musical instrument, take up tai chi, run a marathon, volunteer, or grow your own fruit and vegetables. This is all positive, but make sure to work on other pillars also. It is not uncommon for gamblers to replace one addiction with another, and although the new activity may not be as damaging as gambling, it is important to maintain balance in life and develop and spend time on all pillars equally.

6.2.1 Emotional pillar

This is vitally important. We have touched on how to cope with moods, impulses, and negative emotional states previously. Some useful practices here include:

- Rest: get ample, restful, and reenergising sleep. Follow some simple rules such as keeping your bedroom clean, uncluttered, dark, and at a comfortable temperature, wear comfortable clothing, avoid eating large meals in the evening, and avoid coffee, sugar, and alcohol at least three hours before bed. If necessary, it might be worth considering a natural sleep aid such as valerian.
- Meditation and mindfulness practice: these activities help calm the mind from the torrent of thoughts and they help bring calmness into one's life; they also aid in the reduction of stress.
- Acknowledge your emotions, observe your emotions but do not get caught up with the feelings and thoughts they conjure up. Just reflect on them, be present, do not resist but embrace them as part of who you are, do not act on them, become a non-judgemental observer of your thoughts and emotions, and let them be a motivation for personal growth and development.
- Avoid being impulsive. Delay gratification, stop being self-indulgent, face up to your responsibilities, and feel your emotional resolve strengthen as a result.
- Healthy diet: what we eat influences how we feel, so eat plenty of natural foods, fruit, vegetables, legumes, whole grains, pulses, and fish that promote a healthy mental state; also, take vitamin, mineral, and health supplements such as omega-3 fish oils, magnesium, iron, and multi-vitamins, which help sustain and maintain healthy mental and emotional states. Reduce or eliminate alcohol, caffeine drinks, fatty foods, and refined white sugar.
- Take up alternative treatments such as yoga, Pilates, reiki, reflexology, acupuncture, tai chi, homeopathy, naturopathy, herbalism, etc.
- Partake in outdoor activities such as walking, cycling, hiking, swimming, gardening, and immersing yourself in nature.
- Avoid negative people and surround yourself with people who add joy, energy, and positivity to your life.

- Do not do things that you do not want to do. Do not be afraid to say no. You may feel obligated to people who helped you on your road to recovery, however, be honest with them if you genuinely feel unable to facilitate a request made by them to you.
- Try and evaluate how you deal with emotions, assess the process and not just the outcome. Once the process is right then over time, even if you do not see immediate results, you will develop the coping skills to properly manage your emotions.
- Reduce or eliminate intake of mind-altering toxins such as alcohol and drugs.
- Addiction counselling or psychotherapy may be an avenue for some people. Cognitive behavioural therapy is deemed an ideal therapy for recovering problem gamblers, as it helps address a lot of the erroneous attitudes and beliefs towards gambling while at the same time helping clients deal with thoughts, urges, and behaviours around gambling; a list of counselling and psychotherapy contacts are outlined in Appendix 7.

6.2.2 Physical pillar

As mentioned previously, the benefits of physical exercise are many: it helps maintain a healthy heart, increases levels of neurotransmitters in the brain (specifically the dopamine system), and releases endorphins in the brain that will help improve mood and a sense of well-being.

Suggested activities that you can do to help build up and fortify your physical pillar:

- Thirty to forty minutes of daily exercise such as walking, jogging, cycling, swimming, or gym workouts. Early on in recovery you will be suffering from a lot of fatigue caused by mental

exhaustion and stress, but try to make sure you get thirty to forty minutes of exercise each day.
- Yoga, Pilates, and Zumba are all good exercises for physical well-being.
- Sufficient rest and a good diet will replace energies expended in exercising, and drinking plenty of water will naturally cleanse the body of toxins.
- Nutrition is very important in maintaining a healthy mind and body. Eat plenty of fresh fruit, vegetables, salads, herbs, and include an adequate amount of fish, meat, and grains in your diet. Omega-3 oils will help improve your mood and mental well-being. Supplementation in the form of vitamin supplements and herbal remedies will help make up for, but are not a replacement for, any deficiencies you have in your diet. Any diet should be a balanced mix of carbohydrates (bread, pasta, cereals, rice, pulses, nuts, fruits and vegetables) and protein (found in dairy produce, eggs, fish, poultry and nuts). Important also to eat sufficient fibre; found in brown bread, brown rice, brown pasta, granola, high fibre cereals, beans, and pulses, adequate amount of vitamins and minerals (magnesium, copper, chromium, calcium, potassium, selenium, and zinc). Drink up to 8 glasses of water spread throughout the day to keep hydrated and help flush out toxins in the body. Try and eat less and more often, and have larger meals earlier in the day, as one's metabolism will burn it off during the day and puts less stress on the body later in the day; when the body needs rest. So have a large breakfast, medium size lunch and light supper. Eat fruit on an empty stomach or well before other meals. Drink herbal teas instead of caffeinated tea or coffee and snack on wholegrain bars or fruit instead of eating biscuits, sweets, ice cream or chocolate. However, no harm to treat yourself and indulge in eating out or having a few glasses of wine now and then; as a reward for your discipline in eating and staying healthy.

- Reduce or eliminate alcohol and cigarettes. Alcohol can reduce your inhibitions and consequently lower your guard against gambling, so be conscious of this if you do partake in drinks at an event. Reduce also the intake of salt, refined white sugar, and caffeine.
- See Appendix 7 for some good nutritional websites that you can reference.

6.2.3 Spiritual pillar

This simply refers to your own spirituality or your true self—who you are and why you are here and finding a spiritual basis for life that is not based on what you own or what you have in the bank. Many people are agnostic, but all people at some point in their lives reflect on their true essence and why they are here on this planet. That is what I am referring to here and not any religious dogma or specific system of beliefs. Years of gambling may have stripped away any purpose or meaning in your life, and your religion up to now was gambling, but your recovery may open up new doors to a spiritual dimension that will bring deeper meaning and purpose to your life. Time away from the hustle and bustle of life to be introspective, to reflect, and be at peace with oneself, will not only bring calmness but will help you discover who you really are. In his book *The Seven Spiritual Laws of Success*, Deepak Chopra states "that success and happiness in life depend on knowing who we really are and that when our internal reference point is our spirit—our true self, not the ego—we experience all the power of our spirit (our true self)."

Some examples of how you can build up your spiritual pillar:

- Attending a religious establishment such as a church, mosque, shrine, synagogue, or temple to silently reflect and

pray, or taking private time away to be still and serene, and to reflect on life.
- Immersing yourself in nature, hiking in forests or mountains, gardening, cycling country roads, fishing, walking by the ocean, and observing all the various activities and intricate ways of nature and the interconnectedness of everything; help in finding the peace of mind and serenity that will nourish your own spirituality.
- Volunteering for community or local help groups; they can help build a sense of perspective on life and add to and nourish your own spirituality.
- Doing a good deed for someone in need or indeed helping other recovering problem gamblers on their journey.

6.2.4 Financial pillar

Managing your finances will take time to master. Refer to "Coping with financial pressures" in phase three of the "SAFEstep™" method, "Functioning and Economy". Debt and financial strain may well take years to stabilise. It can be exhausting and frustrating having limited funds to do anything. However, many enjoyable things in life are free. You will begin to explore new avenues and unearth better, no-cost, ways of enjoying yourself. See the next section (6.2.5), the personal development pillar, for guidance. Please use the financial summary worksheet in appendix 2 regularly; it is about management of debt, and as stated earlier, those who shout the loudest may need it the least.

Make sure you have enough money to cover basic needs first like rent, food, and bills; the rest you can distribute to your creditors. Leave aside emotion when dealing with debt. Prioritise and renegotiate with creditors. Do not let any financial pressure cause you to go back to gambling. If pressure is intense, then seek financial advice from organisations like an insolvency service (see list of organisations in Appendix 7). It is important also to keep all correspondence, e-mails, and letters for future reference. Any verbal agreements need to be followed up in writing. Do not commit to a repayment plan if you are not sure you can meet it. It is better to under commit and over deliver than to over commit and under deliver. Finally, if there is any threat of violence to you or your family, contact the police immediately.

6.2.5 Personal development pillar

This pillar covers a broad spectrum. Abraham Maslow proposed a *Hierarchy of Needs* concept with *Self Acutalisation (Personal Development)* at the top, defined as: "The desire to become more and more what one is, to become everything that one is capable of becoming." You will identify what you would like to do once your life is free from the throes of a pernicious gambling addiction. You have within you the power to be all you want to be. The advice here is to be brave and do those productive things that you feel like doing, and never mind if they do not fit into the norms of your friends or family—it is your life. Try also to set realistic attainable goals, and do not try to achieve something difficult in a tight timeframe. I would suggest that you set a goal, but break that goal into smaller parts or sub-goals; for example, if you want to learn photography, read up about it online (goal one), then call into a camera shop and pick the brains of the staff on best cameras (goal two), register for a photography class (goal three), and then buy a camera (goal four). This means you have a clear plan with set goals. Another example would be to plan to do a fifty-kilometre charity bicycle ride; then *goal one* would be to get a proper road bike, *goal two* would be to cycle for ten kilometres; to get you going and get used to the bike, *goal three* would be to join a club or cycling group, and *goal four* would be to gradually increase the distance cycled each week, building up fitness each time. Important also to reward yourself when you achieve your goals.

There are many activities and hobbies you can do; some examples include:

- Taking an evening course in anything that interests you; e.g., legal, business, arts and crafts, woodwork, web design, sound engineering, language class, photography, DIY, computers, poetry, journalism, first aid and so on.
- Joining a social group; e.g., hill-walking club, music group, youth club, poetry group, cycling group, historical tours, or choir group.
- Learning something new like DIY, musical instrument, self-defence, a foreign language, taking up a new career, a new role at work, or moving to a new location.
- Read up on the psychology, astronomy, astrology, biology, and history topics that you were always interested in but never gave time to.
- Raise funds for a charity.
- Volunteer your time and services to a worthy cause.

6.2.6 Social network pillar

Gambling may well have impacted negatively on your relationships with family, friends, and your social network. This is understandable, as up to now your only serious relationship was with gambling. You may have developed close friendships with fellow gamblers and these relationships may now be no longer sustainable. Returning to the same environment as before could lead to a relapse to gambling. Family and friends may have distanced themselves from you, and you may feel very isolated. However, see this as an opportunity to rebuild your social network. By working on your personal development pillar you will be automatically building up a network of friends; these friendships will be built on solid foundations and will endure.

Many social events do not involve spending money or having to go as a group or couple, seek them out and take a leap of faith. You will be rewarded and will uncover interests, events, and people who will add much joy, happiness, and variety to your life. Social websites like www.meetup.com are an excellent way to join people, with similar interests, in undertaking activities such as hiking, playing music, theatre going, visiting museums, book reviews, and so on. Self-pity and lack of motivation may stop you from engaging in social activities; put all perceptions, prejudices, and biases aside and push the boundaries of your comfort zone; a whole new life awaits you.

6.2.7 Relationship pillar

The gambling addiction may have cost or damaged your relationship with your spouse, partner, friends, or family members. In many cases relationships can be repaired and are stronger and better as a result. In many cases, gambling will have eroded the trust and love that existed between the gambler and his or her spouse or partner. The consequences may be that your relationship is now irrevocably damaged and cannot be recovered. It may be difficult to accept this and you may be expending a lot of energy trying to salvage the relationship. Refer to phase two and "Acceptance", this will help you move on and deal better with the feelings of guilt and emotional pain that you are enduring.

You cannot change how your partner thinks or reacts, so by insisting that she or he takes you back will only make matters worse. Concentrate on building up your pillars, and over time you may well find your "true love", or you may rebuild the relationship with your former partner or spouse. Remember, another person will not make you fulfilled, complete, or salvage you. Only you can make yourself fulfilled, happy, and complete and no one else. Fear, neediness, and longing for company and happiness drive many people to seek out relationships; purely for the sake of being in one. The Indian yogi and mystic Sadhguru once said, "If you're happy by your own nature, now relationships will become a means for you to express your happiness not to seek happiness."

Communication in any relationship is key to making it a success. Relationship issues often arise because couples do not communicate their needs, wants, hopes and anxieties to each other. Provide constructive feedback to each other, not minor issues, but about matters that are important. Do not let issues build up and above all be honest with each other. If the relationship is unsalvageable or the feelings of trust and caring have all but dissipated, then would be best to move on with each other's lives. However, the crisis and your recovery through gambling addiction may strengthen the bonds between you, so give things a chance; it takes time to rebuild your relationship and repair the damage done. If your budget allows, I would recommend you see a relationship or marriage guidance counsellor, this will help explore issues such as how your addiction impacted on your significant other, unexpressed issues and concerns, guidance on how best to address these issues, and how to become more communicative and honest with each other.

All relationships (social, personal, work, and family) can be demanding and require you to give and sacrifice things to make them enduring and successful. It is give and take, however if you feel you are doing all the giving and get nothing back, then re-evaluate what this person adds to your life. If nothing, then possibly time to move on or reduce contact with that person.

You may feel incomplete being single, but being single has many benefits also. You will have more time to partake in activities you enjoy, gives you time and space to rediscover who you really are, and provide you the necessary space to concentrate wholeheartedly on your recovery. If you re-enter a relationship with a former spouse or partner or start a new relationship, enter with an open mind, accept and embrace the differences that exist between you and your partner, cherish and respect your partner, partake in events and activities together, solve problems together, give each other space, become friends, communicate openly with each other, be responsible for your own happiness, and above all work at it.

CHAPTER 7
Help for Partners, Friends, or Family of a Gambling Addict

7.1 Introduction

Gamblers are notoriously adept at hiding their destructive addiction. Their craft and skills of deception are honed over a long period of time. Outwardly the gambler may appear fine, happy, and in control. As the old adage states, "Do not be deceived by appearances." When the gambler reveals his or her addiction or is found out, it is usually a complete shock to those closest to him or her.

I will use the term partner to describe a spouse, girlfriend, boyfriend, family member, friend, or colleague of the problem gambler.

The main objectives of this chapter are:

- Help the partner identify behaviours that may indicate a gambling addiction or gambling problem.
- Teach the partner how to cope with the gambler's behaviours and problems caused by the gambler's addiction.
- Teach the partner what not to do, that is, what actions or attitudes will exacerbate problems or cause the gambler to gamble even more.

The gambler's behaviours may have an inordinate adverse effect on the gambler's partner and family. These problems can include neglect of the family's needs, extreme financial difficulties, impact on mental and emotional well-being of the partner and children of the gambler, total loss of trust between the partner and the gambler, social isolation due to the shame and ignominy of the gambler's actions, health issues, domestic violence, impact on sexual relations due to loss of libido of gambler, and legal issues, to name but a few.

However, the partner and family of a gambler can play a significant role in the gambler's recovery, and the support and motivation offered by the partner can have a very positive impact on treatment success and sustaining the problem gambler's recovery.

It is important to note that while the partner and family can play a significant role in the recovery programme, caution needs to be exercised in terms of what form that support takes. For example, lending money to a gambler can help sustain the gambler's addiction, downplaying or minimising the gambler's destructive behaviours will only lead to the gambler thinking this behaviour is accepted and he or she can continue gambling, and making excuses for the gambler will only pass the burden from the gambler to the partner. Partners can also assume too much responsibility for the gambler and assume the roles and responsibilities that the gambler should be performing, such as minding the children or doing household tasks.

7.2 Stages of stopping

A model has been developed by Professor Carlo DiClemente and James Prochaska that describes the different stages of change involved in stopping problem behaviours. The stages are:

- Pre-contemplation: Not yet acknowledging that there is a problem behaviour that needs to be changed. Gamblers are not aware of the negative consequences, risks, or effects of their gambling. The gambler has no intention to decrease or discontinue gambling.

- Contemplation: Acknowledging that there is a problem but not yet ready or sure of wanting to make a change. They would like to stop gambling but still like to gamble and see more advantages to gambling than not gambling. Considering making changes but with some cautious resistance.
- Preparation/Determination: Getting ready to change. The gambler is aware that the disadvantages of gambling outweigh the benefits. At this point, the gambler may indicate his or her intention to stop gambling to his or her partner. The gambler is thinking about how to cope with changes about to occur in his life.
- Action/Willpower: Changing behaviour. In this phase the gambler will take action to stop gambling and start doing alternative activities like golf, gym, or football, or the gambler has attended Gamblers Anonymous. There are many potential issues and crises during this phase.
- Maintenance: Maintaining the behavioural change and avoiding situations, people, or events that may cause him or her to gamble again. He or she thinks about life without gambling and is enjoying the results of this change.
- Relapse: Returning to older behaviours and abandoning the new changes. It may take a few attempts at working through these phases before a gambler successfully stops gambling completely.
- Termination stage: He or she has confidence that he can maintain changes and not revert back to gambling and looks for alternative activities to define his life.

The reason I outlined the phases of change in stopping problem behaviour is to help make the partner aware of what stage the gambler may be at. This will dictate, to some extent, the coping techniques and strategies to be adopted by the partner in dealing with the partner's out-of-control gambling behaviour.

7.3 Gambling behaviours

As mentioned, deception and lies unfortunately are the hallmarks of a problem gambler. It is almost impossible to detect that a partner may be gambling heavily, especially now with the easy accessibility to betting mediums such as online betting and mobile application betting—gambling has never been made easier. There is a bookmaker in almost every corner of every town in the land; bingo halls, casinos, slot machines, lotto terminals, and scratch card stalls are omnipresent; there is no escape.

To help partners understand when their partners may have a gambling problem, I have listed some behaviours or attitudes that can act as symptoms:

- Becomes restless or irritable at certain times, especially for no apparent reason; this may coincide with race meetings, greyhound races, football, or other major sport events.
- Becomes increasingly defensive of his or her gambling.
- Becomes secretive over money and finances with increased need to control all household finances.
- Makes rather inane excuses to "pop" out for five minutes but does not return for an hour or two.
- Spends a lot of time online at evening or morning and gets annoyed or angry if he or she is intruded upon.
- Uses his or her mobile phone excessively; this may indicate he or she is accessing the mobile betting applications.
- Suffers from physical health problems such as headaches, backache, insomnia, and gastrointestinal problems. While independently may not be an indicator of problem gambling, combined with other behaviours it may be a sign that your partner has a gambling problem.
- Reduces amount of time spent on social activities or with family or friends.

- Demonstrates rather erratic mood swings; for example, one day he or she can be overly nice, confident, happy, and polite and the next day is distant, bored, depressed, and moody.
- Loses control of temper rather easily and carries out violent acts on you or property.
- Buys extravagant presents to make up for missing an important event or buying presents for no apparent reason (this could be to salve his or her conscience for gambling heavy).
- Asks for money out of the blue, making up rather dubious excuses such as leaving the credit card at work or salary payment delayed this week.
- Is restless and unable to sleep, tossing and turning in bed, and totally disinterested in sex, and showing little or no affection.
- Gets annoyed easily if asked to do a basic chore like collecting the children from school.
- Turns phone off for hours on end, is not easily contactable, and when contacted gives no valid reason or offers a dubious excuse for not being contactable.
- Colleagues at work may notice that he or she takes prolonged lunch breaks, takes unexplained or poorly excused absences from work, regularly arrives late for work, talks excessively about the near misses or big wins he or she has had when gambling recently, and has become distant or irritable over the last while for no apparent reason.
- Friends may notice that the gambler has asked for a loan of money on numerous occasions with the promise to pay back but has not done so. If successive loans are given without any effort to repay them, then this would be a cause for concern and indicative of problem gambling.
- Lots of betting receipts in the garbage, bookies' pencils or biros strewn over the house.
- Makes innocuous comments such as "should have backed that horse" or "knew that team would win" out of the blue.

- Dereliction of personal appearance and health, eating unhealthily, not caring about what clothes he or she wears or how he or she looks, not concerned with domestic duties like cleaning, washing, and so on.
- Bank statements are not arriving at house when they should, or he or she is the first to open bank statements and discards them quickly.

The signs and behaviours of a gambling addiction almost mimic those of people having an affair, but in this case the lover is gambling—it is gambling who seduces your partner and who covets his or her time and attention.

7.4 Dealing with problem gamblers

By now, having read this and the previous chapters, you may have a better idea of the causes of problem or pathological gambling, the stages involved in stopping problem gambling behaviour, and the signs of problem gambling.

It is not uncommon for the partner, family, or friends of problem gamblers to blame themselves for the gambler's problem. For example, "I am too busy with work and kids to pay my husband more care and attention; no wonder he gambles." In some cases the partner may be inadvertently feeding or enabling the gambler's gambling by denying that the partner has a gambling problem, and refusing to discuss the issue with others when it arises. The partner may minimise the effect of the gambler's behaviour with excuses such as "Sure, he is entitled to a few bets now and then, and what harm is it causing?"

The motivation of the problem gambler to stop gambling will vary depending on the stage he or she is in (see stages of stopping above), and the strategies to be adopted will vary with each stage. However, for the purposes of simplicity, I have detailed below some coping strategies that can be adopted for all stages of change.

7.5   Coping techniques in dealing with problem gamblers

- First and foremost, it is important to ensure that the gambler bears the full responsibility and consequences for his or her gambling behaviour. While the temptation to assume some or the entire burden for your partner's behaviour may exist, doing so will not allow the gambler to deal directly with his or her gambling addiction and will prevent, in the longer term, a full recovery. Please refer to phase 2, "Acceptance," of the recovery programme for guidance here.
- Once you deem that your partner has a gambling problem, it is important not to threaten or confront him or her; this will only worsen the situation and distance the gambler from you. The best technique here would be to reassure the gambler you care for and love him or her but are concerned about his or her gambling, and are willing to support his or her attempts to stop. Give some examples where the gambler's behaviour negatively affected your relationship, such as "Last week you came home late and missed putting the kids to bed; it upset me and them," or "I miss your company, and you seem to spend a lot of your free time online playing poker instead of being with me," or "I hope you do not mind me asking, but the lads at work are worried that a dear person to them is spending a lot of time out of office, seems distant and moody, and is asking for short term loans a lot. We are there for you and want to see the old you back; want to chat about it?"
- Chat openly, calmly, and honestly about the disadvantages of gambling, such as how much time and money is wasted to the detriment of time spent with family and friends, social

- events, sporting events, and leisure activities. Be supportive and understanding, and mention the avenues open to the gambler to help him or her stop.
- Even after being open and supportive, if the gambling persists, then lay down certain conditions that, if not adhered to, will result in the end of your relationship, friendship, or work contract. Examples of such conditions include: that all credit and debit cards are controlled by you, all bank statements are analysed for large withdrawals, that time spent online in any day is limited to ten to fifteen minutes to check and respond to e-mails or indeed is disallowed completely, and that responsibilities are shared equally. Be open and frank about gambling urges or relapses that the gambler has and discuss steps to prevent them in the future.
- Work through this recovery programme with the gambler, be an active participant, and encourage and give praise as he or she works through the programme. It is just as important for you, as well as the gambler, to understand what triggers cause gambling urges in the gambler, what coping techniques are available (Phase One, "Stability"), and where to go for help.
- Resist the urge to blame the gambler for all your current problems and predicaments. Yes, he or she is solely to blame, but to ensure and sustain recovery, the less confrontation the gambler has to endure, the better. The gambler will undoubtedly be pressured into repaying money to many people, and the financial techniques outlined in phase three, "Functioning and Economy," of the recovery programme will be of immense assistance here.
- Avoid micromanagement of the gambler's journey through the recovery programme or being overly inquisitive about how he or she is coping; this can be too overbearing for the gambler.
- Continue to motivate and support the gambler. Organise little treats after the completion of each phase of the gambling

recovery programme and look at doing joint activities like cycling, tennis, jogging or walking together, playing bridge, movies, or attending theatre together.
- If there is a slip or lapse, then reassure the gambler that this happens and agree on a plan of action to ensure that the gambler quickly gets back on the road to recovery.
- Accept that your partner has a gambling problem and do not deny the existence of the problem to yourself, family members, or others.
- Recovery will take time; be patient and accept that problems caused by the gambler's behaviour may take some time to be rectified.
- If there is domestic or emotional abuse, relationship issues, sexual issues, or financial difficulties, then I recommend you seek professional counselling. See Appendix 7 for a list of agencies and counsellors.
- Support groups like GamAnon can offer great advice and will help you in managing your partner's recovery from his or her gambling addiction.

CHAPTER 8
The Future

I sincerely hope you have come through the thirty days of the recovery programme. You will be more composed and better able to deal with the problems and challenges that will come down the line. If I said, "I guarantee that after thirty days everybody who completes the course will never gamble again," then I would be naive in the extreme. However, if you do relapse, simply start again. I purposefully did not mention this earlier, as I think that giving the idea that it is OK to gamble during the programme and just start again might lead to most people never finishing the programme. Smokers always say, "After my next birthday," or "After Christmas or New Year's, I will try again to stop smoking." That day never comes, so give everything you have to each attempt while sincerely hoping it takes only one attempt. It may be three or thirty-three years since your last bet, but it can be only a second away from your next, so why waste all that hard work in getting where you are today by gambling again? If you do slip, then start from phase one again and strengthen the coping techniques in the area which caused you to relapse, for example, financial strain. But if you set the intention from the core of your being to never gamble again, that unwanted slip will never come to pass. Important also, not to believe that you are at the mercy of an incurable disease and that the threat of gambling will hang over you like "the Sword of Damocles" for the rest of your life. That is living in fear and serves no purpose whatsoever. You have broken free from the clutches of a gambling addiction and it no longer has any power over you. Enjoy and immerse yourself in the great beauty, joy, and mystery of life.

Here are some thoughts on my own recovery. It is not a smooth path. Money issues will persist for some time, but they will abate. During the tough times, say to yourself, "I do not gamble today, and one day I will be debt free"—and one day you will be. Accepting the situation you find yourself in is not always easy, but I have learned to accept my lot in life and realise that this is all part of a journey. Johnny Cash once said in an interview, referring to his own addiction troubles, "I miss the madness." I won't deny that there was a sense of thrill and excitement at times amidst the madness of gambling. But I think what Cash really meant was that the chaos and mayhem of our lives keep us away from finding out who we really are, and with no madness in your life, you have to face yourself and reality. That is initially difficult, but after a time it is enlightening. Get to know yourself; the most profound relationship you will ever have is with yourself, so you might as well get to know who you are and above all enjoy the discovery.

As the layers of your old self, The Gambler, slowly peel away and you are getting more in tune with who you really are, you will undoubtedly face many fears, doubts, insecurities and may feel vulnerable. Embrace your fears and doubts, love them, and be compassionate with them. In his book *Travelling Light*, Daniel O'Leary states that "As with anger, once we enlist and utilise the energy of fear in our favour, we move along our path to wholeness with swifter feet." Do not let fear or doubt imprison you. It may take some time to gain confidence, but do not be afraid to make mistakes; do not be afraid to do new things, meet new people, travel to new places, change careers, or move to a new location. Gambling has imprisoned you for long enough. You have unlocked the door of your cell and are out of that prison now. Enjoy the freedom, you have suffered enough.

Gambling can strip you of your emotions and literally wipe out the enthusiasm for certain things that you once had. Your outlook on life can be less rosy, your energy levels can be depleted, and your general mood can be low. It takes time to rebuild your life. You literally have to deconstruct the gambler and reconstruct your new self. However, you are working with a core person who got hidden under the layers of mayhem and emotional torment of gambling, so it's not as difficult as building from scratch. You will become more appreciative of certain things that you overlooked while gambling, like that extra time spent with your family, partner, and friends; more appreciative of the value of money; and more aware of people in need and how you can help them overcome their difficulties. You will have far less stress and no more need to lie or deceive people—that in itself will bring huge relief.

I do not look back with regret. I used to, and it served no purpose whatsoever. All we have is the now, so immerse yourself in this moment. Let the past be, the future will take care of itself. Try new things, shake it up, and push yourself that bit more. Go to that event you were thinking of, pick up that instrument you were keen on playing as a kid, take up a new sport, join a writers' club, write that book, do that night course you thought of doing but never did, pursue that degree, go fishing, go cycling, give your family your love and time, help a recovering problem gambler, volunteer—I could go on forever. Also, do not take yourself or things too seriously, of course you are dealing with serious issues, but bring humour and joy into your life which will help disarm and dispel a lot of the bad energy and negative emotions that prevail. Humour is a great antidote for stress and anxiety, and yes laughter is the best medicine, so smile, laugh, and as Bobby McFerrin sang "Don't Worry, Be Happy".

We are all human with all the same frailties, self-doubts, concerns and vulnerabilities, so do not be deceived by appearances—we all need a helping hand. To receive anything in life, you need to learn to give first: give people a helping hand when you know they need it, give blessings to those who come into good fortune or have found love and happiness, give your time to good causes, give all your love and time to those closest to you, but expect nothing in return. It may be that you receive nothing other than a positive feeling and sense of humility and graciousness, feelings that have eluded you for years;

that in itself is enough. Life will have its share of ups and downs, and once you give up gambling, you will begin to participate wholly and completely in all life has to offer—this eluded you when you gambled. Be grateful when life is good and be gracious when life is difficult, and know that bad as well as good times pass. Remind yourself in both good and bad times, as the proverb states, "This too shall pass."

Be present and be mindful in everything you do. Your mind will race with thoughts, but as you practice anchoring yourself in the now and putting your focus and attention into the present moment, this will help calm your mind. Distance yourself from your thoughts, emotions, sensations, the mental noise and chatter, and the repetitive painful thoughts. Observe and accept your thoughts, sensations and emotions, but do not judge, resist, act, follow, or concentrate on them; just let them be—be a spectator and not an active participant. Your thoughts are just a sequence of mental events. They are not you. You will have times of mental turbulence and anguish as your mind races with negative thoughts. However, this is a good time to step back and observe your thoughts, emotions, sensations, and behavioural reactions. The more you do this, the less your mind will race.

I found that once I set good intentions—for example, writing this book—all manner of people, things, and events worked in my favour. Have faith in your own abilities, and as you persevere in doing good, you will receive all the power, energy, and resoluteness needed to achieve whatever your intention is. The poet, politician, and writer Johann von Goethe wrote, "If one definitely commits oneself, then Providence moves too. All sorts of things occur to help one that would never otherwise have occurred. A whole stream of events issues from the decision, raising in one's favour all manner of unforeseen incidents and meetings and material assistance, which no man could have dreamed would have come his way. Whatever you can do, or dream you can do, begin it. Boldness has genius, power, and magic in it. Begin it now."

The most valuable thing you will offer anyone is your true self, not the representation of yourself through material objects; they all pass, but your true self is constant. You are already a perfect and wonderful person of infinite value and worth, and possess everything you need within you; you just need to discover it. Dare to dream, and commit wholeheartedly, fearlessly, and courageously in pursuit of your dreams, the universe will help you—have trust in it, but unless you set the intention it will never happen. Show the world who you really are and what you can do, do not let the perceptions, beliefs, emotions, and opinions of others stop or hinder you, and take responsibility for your own life. The only obstacles to your success, happiness and peace of mind are those that you construct yourself. Alexander Dumas wrote, "Misfortune shines a light on the treasures of the intellect." Well, that light is shining brightly on you now. Use your intellect for good, give without expecting anything in return, forgive those who have hurt you, embrace your fears, show compassion instead of anger to those who make your life difficult, believe in yourself, appreciate yourself and the valuable contribution you can make to the world, be proud of who you are, do not take things personally, be happy for what you have and never mind what you don't have, and above all, never ever gamble again. I wish you all the success and blessings on your journey. Take care. Pádraig

APPENDIX 1
Daily Diary Template

Please note all templates used in the book can be downloaded from the following website: www.how-to-stop-gambling.com.

Time	Activity
Morning activities	
1	Wash, breakfast, five minutes visualisation practice
2	Walk on beach
3	Go to town, attend GA meeting, or go to work
Afternoon activities	
4	Lunch
5	Meet friend
6	Go to library
Evening activities	
7	Read phase one of recovery programme
8	Prepare evening meal
9	Watch some TV
	Good night's sleep is essential

Daily Diary Template

Time	Activity
Morning activities	
1	
2	
3	
Afternoon activities	
4	
5	
6	
Evening activities	
7	
8	
9	

APPENDIX 2
Financial Summary Template

1. Total Debt		Priority	3. Basic Living Expenses per month (must meet)		5. Debt Repayment Schedule: Month 1	
Debt Description	Amount		Debt Description	Amount	Name	Amount
Bank Loan + any arrears	€30,000	2	Food	€400	John Doe	€120
Credit Union Loan + any arrears	€10,000	2	ESB and other utilities	€350	Money Lender	€200
John Doe	€5,000	1	Rent or mortgage	€1,120	Bank	€250
Jimmy Smith	€200	3	Diesel	€150		
Money Lender	€2,400	1	Parking	€50		
Car loan + any arrears	€3,000	2	Bus fare	€50	Total	€570
Credit Card	€8,000	2	Cigarettes	€80		
Total	€58,600		Total Outgoings	€2,200		
2. Total Income per month			4. Amount able to pay back per month			
Description	Amount					
Salary	€2,300		Total Income	€2,770		
Social Welfare			Total expenditure	€2,200		
Children's allowance						
Pension	€470		Funds free to pay back	€570		
Total Income	€2,770					

Financial Summary Template

1. Total Debt		Priority	3. Basic Living Expenses (must meet)		5. Debt Repayment Schedule: Month 1	
Debt Description	Amount		Debt Description	Amount	Name	Amount
					Total	
Total			Total Outgoings			
2. Total Income			4. Amount able to pay back per month			
Description	Amount					
			Funds free to pay back			
Total Income						

APPENDIX 3
Managing Urges Template

Example

Day	Trigger	Action	Feelings
Monday	Got paid	Made sure I had no access to credit cards or debit cards, paid off all core bills, and transferred monies to creditors.	I felt good as I suppressed the urge to gamble and paid off some of my creditors.
Tuesday	Bored	Evaluated all activities that I could do. Decided to go and play golf with a friend.	Enjoyed the day with a friend and above all did not gamble, so a day farther down the road in my recovery.
Wednesday	None	Felt good today but kept reviewing the coping techniques of the "Functioning and Economy" phase of the recovery programme.	Feeling happy and beginning to enjoy recovery—in spite of challenges.
Thursday	Argument with partner	Practiced meditation and mindfulness techniques and kept calm.	Initially felt angry and down, but after calming myself with meditation techniques, I felt nice and relaxed.
Friday	Friends going to race meeting	Made my excuses that I have an alternative arrangement and went to two GA meetings that day.	Felt strong and proud not succumbing to request to go gambling. Also, felt secure in company of fellow recovering problem gamblers.

Saturday	Racing on TV	Left on TV and felt relieved that I can look at this and not want to go gambling, and recalled the miserable times I had losing money by betting on very same races before.	Felt bit anxious and worried that I would not be able to handle urge to go gambling, but imagining the horrid times of previous days of heavy losses helped quell the urge.
Sunday	None	Felt nice and relaxed today, and spent lovely time with my family.	Felt so happy being with family and proud am working hard on my recovery, and that I am there for my family, and not stuck in the bookies.

Managing Urges Template

Day	Trigger	Action	Feelings
Monday			
Tuesday			
Wednesday			
Thursday			
Friday			
Saturday			
Sunday			

APPENDIX 4
Problem-Solving Worksheet

Identify the problem	I need to €2,000 to pay a debt.
Define the problem	I need to pay off €2,000 to pay a debt to a friend, Mary, who wants to buy a new car.
Evaluate all options	
Option 1	Take up a second job.
Issue(s)	Have little spare time, as I'm doing a night course that is important to me.
Option 2	Go to Credit Union for a loan.
Issue(s)	Recently got a loan and agreed to keep repayments up again for six months before any other loan requests are made.
Option 3	Talk frankly with Mary and ask if she would accept €400 a month for next five months.
Issue(s)	May mean Mary cannot buy a car for a while.
Decision and outcome	Mary was OK with the arrangement and she got a low-interest loan and bought a car, knowing that I would be paying back her loan over next five months. Lesson learned: easier to talk frankly with people about the situation than put myself under immense pressure and possible relapse to gambling.

Problem-Solving Worksheet Template

Identify the problem	
Define the problem	
Evaluate all options	
Option 1	
Issue(s)	
Option 2	
Issue(s)	
Option 3	
Issue(s)	
Decision and outcome	

APPENDIX 5
Benefit Analysis Sheet

No	Benefits of continuing to gamble	Benefits of not gambling
1		
2		
4		
5		
6		
7		
8		
9		
10		

APPENDIX 6

Emotional Analysis Worksheet

Cause	Effect	Action
You are bored, feel in bad humour and have low mood.	Feeling bored and depressed at having nothing to do can cause urges to gamble. Your rationale is that gambling, in spite of losses, gave you some excitement and something to do during the day.	**Step back** from the feelings of boredom and low mood. Sit and relax and observe the feelings you have. Notice how the urge to gamble wells up in you and convinces you that gambling is the antidote to your stress. **Identify** the root cause: The main reason for this is that you are not preoccupying yourself with anything else, other than thinking about gambling and feeling sorry for yourself. **Rationalise:** Yes, anybody who does not partake in activities (not gambling) will find that time drags and will become frustrated at having nothing to do. Where a vacuum and space is created; negative thoughts seed and grow. Would you expect otherwise? The most logical next step is to evaluate options other than gambling, for example, cycling, learning a musical instrument, gym, going for a jog, and so on.

Emotional Analysis Worksheet

Cause	Effect	Action
		Step back **Identify** the root cause: **Rationalise:**

APPENDIX 7
List of Organisations in Ireland, UK, United States and Australia

Organisations in Ireland

Addiction

www.gamblersanonymous.ie   **Tel: 01-8721133**

Gamblers Anonymous (GA) is a fellowship of men and women who share their experience, strength, and hope with each other to solve their common problem and help others recover from a gambling problem.

www.alcoholicsanonymous.ie   **Tel: 01-8420700**

Alcoholics Anonymous is a fellowship of men and women who share their experience, strength, and hope with each other to solve their common problem and help others to recover from alcoholism. The only requirement for membership is a desire to stop drinking.

www.na-ireland.org   **Tel: 01-6728000**

Narcotics Anonymous (NA) is a non-profit fellowship of men and women for whom drugs have become a major problem.

www.gamblersanonymous.ie/gamanon/gamanon.html

Gam-Anon is a fellowship of men and women who are husbands, wives, relatives, or close friends of gamblers who have been affected by the gambling problem.

www.al-anon-ireland.org
The Al-anon 12 Step program of recovery is adapted from Alcoholics Anonymous and is based upon the Twelve Steps, Twelve Traditions, and Twelve Concepts of Service. The Purpose of Al-anon is to help families and friends of alcoholics recover from the effects of living with the problem drinking of a relative or friend in an anonymous environment

www.cuanmhuire.ie
A charitable organisation founded by Sister Consilio Fitzgerald in 1965. It provides a comprehensive structured, abstinence-based residential programme dealing with alcohol, gambling, and drug addiction.

www.how-to-stop-gambling.com
This is a complementary resource to "How to Stop Gambling in 30+1 Days" book where users can download templates, read blogs, view videos etc.

Financial

www.mabs.ie   **Tel: 0761 07 2000**
The Money Advice and Budgeting Service (MABS) is the only free, confidential, independent, and nonjudgmental service in Ireland for people in debt or in danger of getting into debt.

www.moneyadviser.ie   **Tel: 045 888 904**
Money Adviser is a stand-alone, independent, personal finances advisory firm based in Ireland. Using only qualified financial advisers, they specialise in personal finance issues.

www.nca.ie   **Tel: 1890 432 432**
The National Consumer Agency has expert information and useful tools on consumer rights and personal finance.

www.citizensinformation.ie   Tel: 0761 07 4000
Citizens Information provides information on public services and entitlements in Ireland.

www.isi.gov.ie   Tel: 076 106 4200
The mission of the ISI is to help restore people who are insolvent to solvency in a fair, transparent, and equitable way.

www.consumerhelp.ie
Consumer rights and money advice information website.

www.how-to-stop-gambling.com
Website that is a complement to this recovery programme. Site contains templates, videos, discussion forums, blogs, FAQ's etc.

Legal

www.flac.ie   Tel: 1890 350 250
FLAC is an independent human rights organisation dedicated to the realisation of equal access to justice for all. To this end, it campaigns on a range of legal issues but also offers some basic, free legal services to the public.

www.citizensinformation.ie/en/justice/legal_aid_and_advice/
Tel: 0761 07 4000
Citizens Information provides information on public services and entitlements in Ireland.

www.legalaidboard.ie   Tel: 1890 615 200
The Legal Aid Board provides a professional, efficient, cost-effective, and accessible legal aid and mediation service.

www.lawyer.ie   **Tel: 01 667 1476**
This site provides a user-friendly legal information resource about the law in Ireland.

Mental Health Services

www.mymind.org   **Tel: 076 6801060**
This is a community-based provider of mental health services.

www.pieta.ie   **Tel: 01-6010000**
This is a centre for the prevention of self-harm or suicide.

www.mentalhealthireland.ie   **Tel: 01-284 1166**
This organization provides an information service on issues relating to mental health and mental illness through information factsheets, their website, and directly by telephone, post, and e-mail.

www.aware.ie   **Tel: 01-661 7211**
This organization provides face-to-face, phone, and online support for individuals who are experiencing mild to moderate depression, as well as friends and families who are concerned for a loved one.

www.spunout.ie   **Tel: 01-675 3554**
This is a not-for-profit website created by young people for young people. Their service promotes general well-being and healthy living in order to prevent and positively intervene in harmful behaviour where it occurs amongst young people.

www.headstrong.ie   **Tel: 01-472 7010**
Headstrong is The National Centre for Youth Mental Health, a non-profit organisation supporting young people's mental health in Ireland.

www.yourmentalhealth.ie

This website aims to improve awareness and understanding of mental health and well-being in Ireland.

www.samaritans.org/your-community/samaritans-work-ireland
Tel: 1850 60 90 90

The Samaritans is a national charity that wants to reduce emotional distress and reduce suicidal feelings so that fewer people die by suicide. The Samaritans provides confidential, non-judgemental emotional support, 24 hours a day for people who are experiencing feeling of despair.

www.beatingthebeast.com

Online support community for people with depression and related issues.

www.olagola.org

Ó Lá Go Lá is a Not for Profit Organisation registered in Ireland which was set up to provide supervised support to help reduce suicide, depression and other stress related Illness to service users, who are in need of emotional support and encouragement.

Counselling and Therapy

www.accord.ie   **Tel: 01-5053112**

ACCORD is an Irish voluntary Catholic organisation that aims to promote a deeper understanding of Christian marriage and to offer people the means to safeguard and nourish their marriage and family relationships.

www.relationshipsireland.com   **Tel: 1890 380 380**

This is an Irish counselling agency providing services to those with problems in their personal relationships and related mental health and well-being issues.

www.counsellingdirectory.ie
This is Ireland's largest independent directory of accredited counsellors/psychotherapists and counselling services.

www.irish-counselling.ie   **Tel: 1890 907 265**
This website seeks to identify, develop, and maintain professional standards of excellence in counselling and psychotherapy.

www.solascounselling.com   **Tel: 01-2108101**
Solas offers a humanistic, person-centred approach to counselling and psychotherapy services.

www.gamblingtherapy.org.uk
This is a free online service that provides practical advice and emotional support to people affected by problem gambling.

www.panicaway.com
Counselling service available for sufferers of panic and anxiety attacks.

Dietary Advice

www.nhs.uk/livewell/healthy-eating/Pages/Healthyeating.aspx
NHS Choices is the online "front door" to the NHS. It is the country's biggest health website and gives all the information you need to make choices about your health.

http://circ.ahajournals.org/content/114/1/82.full.pdf
This is a useful article by the American Heart Association on diet and lifestyle recommendations.

www.nutrition.org.uk
This is a website offering dietary and nutritional advice.

www.bhf.org.uk/heart-health/prevention/healthy-eating.aspx
This is a useful dietary and healthy eating article by the British Heart Foundation.

www.eatforhealth.gov.au
Advice about the amount and kinds of foods that we need to eat for health and wellbeing.

www.livestrong.com
A website that offers diet, nutrition and fitness tips for a healthier lifestyle.

Organisations in the United Kingdom

Addiction

www.gamblersanonymous.org.uk   Tel: 020 7384 3040
Gamblers Anonymous (GA) is a fellowship of men and women who share their experience, strength, and hope with each other to solve their common problem and help others recover from a gambling problem.

www.gambleaware.co.uk   Tel: 0808 8020 133
GambleAware aims to promote responsibility in gambling and provide information to help people make informed decisions about their gambling.

www.gamcare.org.uk   Tel: 0808 8020 133
GamCare provides support, information, and advice to anyone suffering through a gambling problem.

www.gamblingtherapy.org.uk
This is a free online service that provides practical advice and emotional support to people affected by problem gambling.

www.alcoholics-anonymous.org.uk   Tel: 0845 769 7555
Alcoholics Anonymous is a fellowship of men and women who share their experience, strength, and hope with each other to solve their common problem and help others to recover from alcoholism. The only requirement for membership is a desire to stop drinking.

www.gamanon.org.uk
Gam-Anon is a fellowship of men and women who are husbands, wives, relatives, or close friends of gamblers who have been affected by the gambling problem.

http://ukna.org/   Tel: 0300 999 1212

Narcotics Anonymous (NA) is a non-profit fellowship of men and women for whom drugs have become a major problem.

www.al-anonuk.org.uk

The Al-anon 12 Step program of recovery is adapted from Alcoholics Anonymous and is based upon the Twelve Steps, Twelve Traditions, and Twelve Concepts of Service. The purpose of Al-anon is to help families and friends of alcoholics recover from the effects of living with the problem drinking of a relative or friend in an anonymous environment

www.how-to-stop-gambling.com

This is a complementary resource to "How to Stop Gambling in 30+1 Days" book where users can download templates, read blogs, view videos etc.

Mental Health Services

www.nhs.uk/NHSEngland/AboutNHSservices/mentalhealthservices/Pages/Overview.aspx

www.nhs.uk/LiveWell/Mentalhealth/Pages/Mentalhealthhome.aspx

NHS Choices is the online "front door" to the NHS. It is the country's biggest health website and gives all the information you need to make choices about your health.

www.mind.org.uk   Tel: 0300 123 3393

This organization provides advice and support to empower anyone experiencing a mental health problem. They campaign to improve services, raise awareness, and promote understanding.

www.samaritans.org

The Samaritans is a national charity that wants to reduce emotional distress and reduce suicidal feelings so that fewer people die by suicide. The Samaritans provides confidential, non-judgemental emotional support, 24 hours a day for people who are experiencing feeling of despair.

www.survive.org.uk

A UK based suicide prevention support group.

www.beatingthebeast.com

Online support community for people with depression and related issues.

www.olagola.org

Ó Lá Go Lá is a Not for Profit Organisation registered in Ireland which was set up to provide supervised support to help reduce suicide, depression and other stress related Illness to service users, who are in need of emotional support and encouragement.

Financial

www.moneyadviceservice.org.uk   **Tel: 0300 500 5000**

The Money Advice Service helps people manage their money. They do this directly through their own free and impartial advice service.

www.financialadvice.co.uk   **Tel: 0800 092 124**

This website offers financial advice by qualified financial professionals.

www.nationaldebtline.co.uk   **Tel: 0808 808 4000**

This is a helpline that provides free confidential and independent advice on how to deal with debt problems.

www.stepchange.org   Tel: 0800 138 1111
   This is a free debt advice service.

www.creditaction.org.uk   Tel: 020 7062 8933
   Credit Action is the United Kingdom's financial capability charity, dedicated to helping people stay on top of their money.

www.insolvency.gov.uk/insolvency/personal-insolvency
   UK's Insolvency Service.

Legal

www.ukfreelegaladvice.com
   This website provides clients with fast, efficient, and, most importantly, high quality legal advice, and assistance tailored to meet the expectations of each individual client.

www.adviceguide.org.uk/england/law_e/law_legal_system_e/law_taking_legal_action_e/help_with_legal_costs.htm#legal_aid_for_criminal_cases
   This is a useful resource that provides information on civil legal aid and legal services.

www.takelegaladvice.com/news-and-information/legal-guidance/-/How-do-I-get-free-advice/
   This website provides guidance on how to obtain free legal advice in the United Kingdom.

Counselling and Therapy

www.samaritans.org   Tel: 08457 90 90 90
   Samaritans is a national charity wanting to reduce emotional distress and reduce suicidal feelings so that fewer people die by suicide.

www.bacp.co.uk   **Tel: 01455 883300**
This is a psychological therapists' register.

www.gordonmoody.org.uk   **Tel: 01384241292**
This website provides advice, education, and high quality and innovative therapeutic support to problem gamblers and those affected by problem gambling.

www.relate.org.uk   **Tel: 0300 100 1234**
Counselling, support and information for all relationships

www.counselling-directory.org.uk
List of qualified and registered counsellors and psychotherapists in the UK.

www.familytherapy.org.uk
A UK family therapy website. Provides information on how to deal with relationship difficulties, marriage problems, divorce and so on.

www.panicaway.com
Counselling service available for sufferers of panic and anxiety attacks.

Dietary Advice

www.nhs.uk/livewell/healthy-eating/Pages/Healthyeating.aspx
NHS Choices is the online "front door" to the NHS. It is the country's biggest health website and gives all the information you need to make choices about your health.

http://circ.ahajournals.org/content/114/1/82.full.pdf
This is a useful article on diet and lifestyle recommendations by the American Heart Association.

www.nutrition.org.uk
This is a website offering dietary and nutritional advice.

www.bhf.org.uk/heart-health/prevention/healthy-eating.aspx
This is a useful dietary and healthy eating article by the British Heart Foundation.

www.eatforhealth.gov.au
Advice about the amount and kinds of foods that we need to eat for health and wellbeing.

www.livestrong.com
A website that offers diet, nutrition and fitness tips for a healthier lifestyle.

Organisations in the United States

Addiction

www.gamblersanonymous.org/ga/hotlines
Tel: (626) 960-3500
Gamblers Anonymous (GA) is a fellowship of men and women who share their experience, strength, and hope with each other to solve their common problem and help others recover from a gambling problem.

www.gamblingtherapy.org
This is a free online service that provides practical advice and emotional support to people affected by problem gambling.

www.aa.org
Alcoholics Anonymous is a fellowship of men and women who share their experience, strength, and hope with each other to solve their common problem and help others to recover from alcoholism. The only requirement for membership is a desire to stop drinking.

www.gam-anon.org **Tel: 718-352-1671**
Gam-Anon is a fellowship of men and women who are husbands, wives, relatives, or close friends of gamblers who have been affected by the gambling problem.

www.na.org
Narcotics Anonymous (NA) is a non-profit fellowship of men and women for whom drugs have become a major problem.7

www.ncpgambling.org **Tel: 1-800-522-4700**
The National Council on Problem Gambling is the national advocate for programs and services to assist problem gamblers and their families.

www.how-to-stop-gambling.com
This is a complementary resource to "How to Stop Gambling in 30+1 Days" book where users can download templates, read blogs, view videos etc.

Mental Health Services

www.mentalhealthamerica.net
Mental Health America, founded in 1909, is the nation's leading community-based network dedicated to helping all Americans achieve wellness by living mentally healthier lives.

www.nafcclinics.org
The National Association of Free and Charitable Clinics (NAFC) is the only non-profit 501c(3) organization whose mission is solely focused on the issues and needs of the more than 1,200 Free and Charitable Clinics and the people they serve in the United States.

www.nami.org
NAMI is the National Alliance on Mental Illness, the nation's largest grassroots mental health organization dedicated to building better lives for the millions of Americans affected by mental illness.

www.findahealthcenter.hrsa.gov/Search_HCC.aspx
Health resources and services administration website.

http://psychcentral.com/lib/telephone-hotlines-and-help-lines/000173
A list of useful telephone hotlines and helplines.

www.depressedlikeme.com
A website that provides an overview of depression, its causes and treatment.

www.olagola.org
Ó Lá Go Lá is a Not for Profit Organisation registered in Ireland which was set up to provide supervised support to help reduce suicide, depression and other stress related Illness to service users, who are in need of emotional support and encouragement.

Financial

www.moneymanagement.org
MMI offers a wide variety of financial services to help improve your financial life. No matter what your financial situation, we can help you to establish a plan of action for achieving your financial goals.

www.usa.gov/topics/money/credit/debt/out-of-control.shtml
Advice on selecting a credit counselling agency.

www.findanadviser.org/find-an-adviser.aspx
This website is run by The Personal Finance Society, the professional body for Financial Advisers. It provides access to appropriately qualified members who commit to the highest professional and ethical standards.

Legal

www.lsc.gov/find-legal-aid
LSC is the single largest funder of civil legal aid for low-income Americans in the nation.

www.dmoz.org/Society/Law/Organizations/Legal_Aid
List of low cost legal aid organisations

Counselling and Therapy

www.samaritansusa.org
Samaritans is a national charity wanting to reduce emotional distress and reduce suicidal feelings so that fewer people die by suicide.

www.panicaway.com
Counselling service available for sufferers of panic and anxiety attacks.

Dietary Advice

www.nhs.uk/livewell/healthy-eating/Pages/Healthyeating.aspx
NHS Choices is the online "front door" to the UK's NHS. It is the UK's biggest health website and gives all the information you need to make choices about your health.

http://circ.ahajournals.org/content/114/1/82.full.pdf
This is a useful article on diet and lifestyle recommendations by the American Heart Association.

www.nutrition.org.uk
This is a website of the British Nutrition Foundation offering dietary and nutritional advice.

www.bhf.org.uk/heart-health/prevention/healthy-eating.aspx
This is a useful dietary and healthy eating article by the British Heart Foundation.

www.eatforhealth.gov.au
Advice about the amount and kinds of foods that we need to eat for health and wellbeing.

www.livestrong.com
A website that offers diet, nutrition and fitness tips for a healthier lifestyle.

Organisations in Australia

Addiction

www.gansw.org.au   **Tel: (02) 9726 6625**

Gamblers Anonymous (GA) is a fellowship of men and women who share their experience, strength, and hope with each other to solve their common problem and help others recover from a gambling problem.

www.gamblingtherapy.org

This is a free online service that provides practical advice and emotional support to people affected by problem gambling.

www.aa.org.au

Alcoholics Anonymous is a fellowship of men and women who share their experience, strength, and hope with each other to solve their common problem and help others to recover from alcoholism. The only requirement for membership is a desire to stop drinking.

www.gansw.org.au/GamAnon.htm

Gam-Anon is a fellowship of men and women who are husbands, wives, relatives, or close friends of gamblers who have been affected by the gambling problem.

www.na.org.au

Narcotics Anonymous (NA) is a non-profit fellowship of men and women for whom drugs have become a major problem.7

www.how-to-stop-gambling.com

This is a complementary resource to "How to Stop Gambling in 30+1 Days" book where users can download templates, read blogs, view videos etc.

Mental Health Services

https://mhsa.aihw.gov.au/home
Mental health services in Australia provides a picture of the national response of the health and welfare service system to the mental health care needs of Australians

www.cmha.org.au/links.html
Links to support groups, community based organisations, State and Territory bodies.

www.mentalhealth.asn.au
Offers information and education advice about protecting mental health, mutual support and advocacy services.

www.healthdirect.gov.au/mental-health-disorders
Offers information and education advice about protecting mental health.

www.depressedlikeme.com
A website that provides an overview of depression, its causes and treatment.

www.olagola.org
Ó Lá Go Lá is a Not for Profit Organisation registered in Ireland which was set up to provide supervised support to help reduce Suicide, Depression and other stress related Illness to service users, who are in need of emotional support and encouragement.

Financial

www.financialcounsellingaustralia.org.au
Financial Counselling Australia (FCA) is the peak body for financial counsellors in Australia.

www.moneysmart.gov.au/managing-your-money/managing-debts/financial-counselling
Information on free financial counselling and organisations that can help.

Legal

www.freelegal.com.au
Online portal to free legal aid information.

www.legalaidact.org.au/aboutus/otherlegalservices/legalaidaustralia.php
Information on legal aid in Australia.

Counselling and Therapy

www.thesamaritans.org.au
Samaritans is a national charity wanting to reduce emotional distress and reduce suicidal feelings so that fewer people die by suicide.

www.suicide.org/hotlines/international/australia-suicide-hotlines.html
List of suicide prevention hotlines in Australia.

Dietary Advice

www.nhs.uk/livewell/healthy eating/Pages/Healthyeating.aspx
NHS Choices is the online "front door" to the UK's NHS. It is the UK's biggest health website and gives all the information you need to make choices about your health.

http://circ.ahajournals.org/content/114/1/82.full.pdf
This is a useful article on diet and lifestyle recommendations by the American Heart Association.

www.nutrition.org.uk
This is a website of the British Nutrition Foundation offering dietary and nutritional advice.

www.bhf.org.uk/heart-health/prevention/healthy-eating.aspx
This is a useful dietary and healthy eating article by the British Heart Foundation.

www.eatforhealth.gov.au
Advice about the amount and kinds of foods that we need to eat for health and wellbeing.

www.livestrong.com
A website that offers diet, nutrition and fitness tips for a healthier lifestyle.

Printed in Great Britain
by Amazon